my first sewing book

my first sewing book

35 easy and fun projects for children aged 7 years old +

Edited by Susan Akass

CICO **kidz**

Published in 2011 by CICO Kidz

An imprint of Ryland Peters & Small

519 Broadway, 5th Floor,
New York NY 10012

20–21 Jockey's Fields,
London WC1R 4BW

www.cicobooks.com

10 9 8 7 6 5 4 3 2 1

A CIP catalog record for this book is
available from the Library of Congress
and the British Library.

ISBN: 978-1-907563-71-3

Printed in China

Editor: Susan Akass

Designer: Elizabeth Healey

Illustration: Rachel Boulton and
Hannah George; techniques illustration
by Stephen Dew and Kate Simunek

See page 128 for photography credits.

Contents

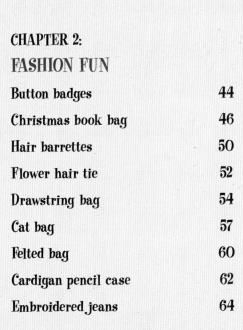

Introduction

Once you have caught the sewing bug there will be no stopping you; you will just want to keep on sewing and this book is full of ideas to help you get creative. In **My First Sewing Book** there are four chapters—Terrific Toys, Fashion Fun, Delightful Decorations, and Gifts and Cards. The materials you use to make them need not be expensive—many projects in the book are made by reusing old clothes. So make sure no clothes, even odd socks or shrunken woolens, get thrown away in your family before you have checked them out for possible ideas!

To help you get started, we have graded all the projects with one, two, or three smiley faces. The level one projects are the easiest. The stitches used are very simple and there is not much sewing to do. The level two projects use some different stitches and are a little longer, but they are still quite easy. The level three projects are a bit more challenging, for when your sewing skills are really getting good.

There's a list of all the stitches and techniques you will use at the start of each project and the pages where you can find instructions if you need them. There's also a list of materials. Since many of these are used in lots of the projects, it's good to put together a sewing box that contains the basics.

TOP TIPS

In all projects, remember these top tips:

1. When cutting out patterns, especially rectangles, try to pin them onto the fabric in line with the tiny threads you can see in the fabric (on felt it doesn't matter).

2. When using patterned fabrics, check which is the right side and wrong side of the fabric—you will be able to spot the difference. Be careful to follow instructions about right and wrong sides.

3. Always secure your thread so it doesn't pull out. With yarn (wool) and floss (embroidery thread) tie two knots on top of each other at the end of the thread. When using cotton thread sew a few small stitches on top of one another. Do the same when you finish.

Project levels

○○☺	○☺☺	☺☺☺
Level 1	**Level 2**	**Level 3**
These are very easy: no complex stitches and not much sewing.	These use some more complex stitches and are slightly longer projects, but are still quite easy.	These are longer, more challenging projects that may require some adult help with using an iron.

Your sewing box

We suggest you put together a sewing box that contains:

A pencil

A pen

A ruler

A tape measure

Squared paper (e.g. from a math book) for making patterns

Plain paper for tracing templates

Scissors for cutting paper

Sharp scissors kept especially for cutting fabric

Pins

Needles, including some big ones with big eyes

A needle threader (this will save you a lot of time!)

Cotton thread, embroidery floss (thread), and yarn (wool) in different colors

Fiberfill (stuffing)

Glue

Pinking shears

You also need to start a collection of different materials, so look out for:

Buttons—especially pretty ones. Cut them off clothes that are too worn out to pass on or look out for boxes of them in charity stores and garage sales.

Ribbons and braids—look out for them on gifts or on boxes of chocolate. They will always come in useful.

Fabrics—some you will have to buy, but often, small leftover pieces (remnants) are sold very cheaply. A collection of different-colored felts is a must and you can buy these at craft shops or online. Remember to save pieces of fabric from clothes that are too worn out to pass on and keep leftover scraps from other projects. Ask any adult stitchers you know to keep any leftover fabric for you. They are sure to want to encourage a new stitcher!

CHAPTER ONE

Terrific toys

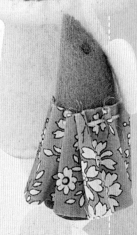

Juggling animals

Have hours of fun learning how to juggle with these animal juggling balls—you can make a rabbit, a mouse, a chicken, and a dog. Fill them with dried lentils or dried peas to make them the right weight for perfect juggling. Try starting with two balls and once you can juggle with these, make another to build up your animal family!

In this project, you will use:

Backstitch (see page 115)

Using a pattern (see page 114)

You will need:

Squared paper and a pencil

A ruler

Scissors

Fabric (recycle worn-out clothes!)

Felt

Pins

A needle and thread

Large lentils or dried peas

A spoon

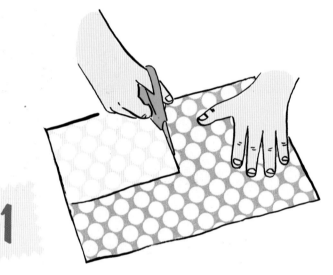

1

Cut out a square with sides 5½ inches (14 cm) long on the squared paper. Use this as a template to cut out two squares of fabric for each animal. If you can, choose a different fabric for each animal.

2

Photocopy the templates on page 125 at double the size, then cut out paper patterns for the features needed for each animal. Pin the paper shapes onto felt and cut them out. Remove the pins and pattern pieces.

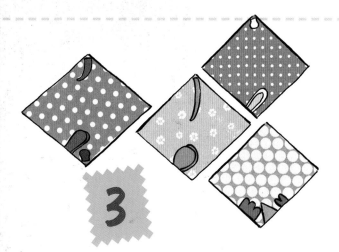

3

Place down one square of fabric right side up. Arrange the felt decorations on the fabric as shown in the diagram.

4

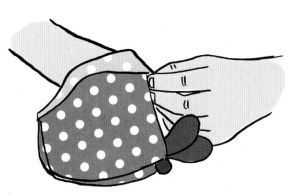

Place the other square of fabric on top of this, right side down (so that the right sides are together). Pin the two sides together, making sure you pin through the felt pieces to hold them in place. Thread a needle, pull the thread through so that it is double, and tie a knot at the end.

5

Stitch around three sides of the fabric, using small backstitches so that the lentils won't fall out. Make sure that you stitch through the felt pieces, too. Secure the thread with a few small stitches at the end. Trim the thread and remove the pins.

6

Turn the fabric bag the right way out. Check that the felt decorations are securely stitched in place.

Throw it up and CATCH IT IF YOU CAN!

7 Fill the bag about three-quarters full of lentils or dried peas.

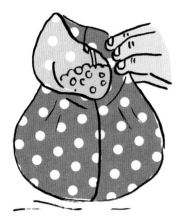

8 To finish the beanbag, turn in the open sides by about ½ inch (1 cm).

9 Pin the two open sides together to make a pyramid shape. Push the tail into the middle of this seam and pin it in position. Thread your needle with another double thread and knot it. Stitch the two sides together with more small backstitches, making sure that you stitch through the tail. Finish the stitching with a few small stitches to secure the thread firmly.

Wise old owl

This wise old owl is a real hoot! He'll sit on the end of your bed and stare at you with big, friendly eyes. Make him bright and colorful by using one patterned fabric for his body and another for his wings. You could even make him from a favorite worn-out dress or blouse (but ask first).

Twit TWOO!

In this project, you will use:

Backstitch (see page 115)

Slipstitch (see page 117)

Running stitch (see page 115)

Using a pattern (see page 114)

You will need:

Scissors

24 x 11 inches (60 x 30 cm) fabric for the body

Scraps of fabric for the wings

Felt for the feet and feathers

White and black felt for the eyes

Orange felt for the beak

Pins

A needle and thread

Fiberfill (stuffing)

Needle and embroidery floss (thread) in different colors, including black and orange

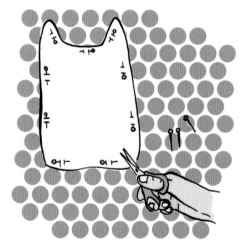

1 Photocopy the templates on page 124 at double the size, then cut out paper patterns for the owl's body, foot, wing, eye, pupil, beak, and feathers. Fold the fabric for the body in half, pin the body pattern to it, and cut around it. Remove the pins and pattern.

2 Pin the two body pieces together, right sides together. Cut a length of thread and thread the needle. Starting with a few small stitches to hold the thread in place, sew the body together with backstitch—but leave the bottom edge open. Finish with a few small stitches. Trim the thread and remove the pins.

3

Turn the body the right way out and stuff with Fiberfill, pushing it well into the ears with the blunt end of a pencil, and then filling the body. Put to one side.

4

Fold the felt for the feet in half, pin the paper pattern for a foot to it, and cut around it. Remove the pins and pattern to give you two feet. Turn the raw edges along the bottom of the owl's body to the inside and put the top of the feet inside the opening. Pin in position. Close the opening with backstitch, starting and finishing with a few small stitches to hold the thread in place. Trim the thread and remove the pins.

5

Fold the fabric for the wings in half, pin the paper pattern for a wing to it, and cut around it. Repeat to give you four wing pieces. Remove the pins and pattern. Pin two wing pieces together, right sides facing.

Starting and finishing with a few small stitches, sew the wing pieces together with backstitch. Leave a 1-inch (2.5-cm) opening in each wing. Turn the wings right way out and stuff with Fiberfil. Tuck the raw edges of fabric inside the wings and close the opening using slipstitch, starting and finishing with a few small stitches.

6

Sew a few stitches onto the owl where one wing will go, then sew through the back of the wing. Sew a few more stitches through the back of the wing and the owl's body until the wing feels firm, then finish with a few small stitches. Trim the thread. Repeat for the other wing.

7

Using the pattern pieces for the eye, cut out two white circles of felt. Using the pattern piece for the pupil, cut out two slightly smaller circles of black felt for the pupils. Starting and finishing with a knot on the back of the white circle, sew a black circle onto the white one with black embroidery floss. Use big stitches to look like eyelashes. Trim the floss. Repeat for the other eye.

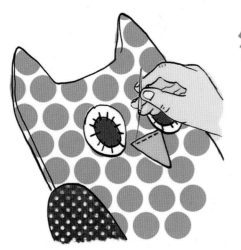

8 Pin the eyes onto the owl. Starting with a few small stitches and using the white thread, sew the first eye in place with running stitch. Push the needle under the fabric to the other eye and stitch this one on, too. Finish with a few small stitches. Remove the pins and trim the thread.

Using the beak pattern piece, cut out a beak from orange felt. Thread the needle with orange floss and, starting and finishing with a knot, sew the beak in place, sewing along the top with a few running stitches.

9 Using the feather pattern piece, cut out three rows of feathers from the felt. Thread your needle with embroidery floss to match the feathers and tie a knot. Sew the bottom row of feathers onto the owl with running stitch. Now trim off one of the four feathers in the next row to leave three. Sew this short row on, overlapping the bottom row and with the three feathers falling in between the four feathers of the first row. Finally, sew on the last row of feathers in line with the bottom row and overlapping the middle row.

T-shirt creatures

Make a cuddly monster friend by recycling a favorite, worn-out T-shirt! If you've got lots of worn-out T-shirts, you can make a whole tribe of monsters with weird and wonderful faces. Let your imagination run wild!

In this project, you will use:

Backstitch (see page 115)

Running stitch (see page 115)

Slipstitch (see page 117)

Sewing on buttons (see page 116)

You will need:

An old T-shirt (check with an adult before you cut one up!)

A felt-tip pen

Pins

Scissors

A needle and thread

Fiberfill (stuffing)

Scraps of felt

Embroidery floss (thread) and a needle

Buttons

Yarn (wool) and a needle with a large eye

1

Turn the T-shirt inside out and lay it flat on the table. Draw the shape for your creature onto it with the felt-tip pen. It will end up smaller when you have sewn it, so draw it bigger than you want it. It can be any shape you want—the crazier, the better! Pin the layers of the T-shirt together and cut out with scissors, making sure you cut through both layers.

2

Cut a length of thread and thread the needle. Starting with a few small stitches, backstitch all the way around your shape about ¾ inch (2 cm) from the edge. Leave an opening of about 2 inches (5 cm) for stuffing. Finish with some more small stitches. Remove the pins.

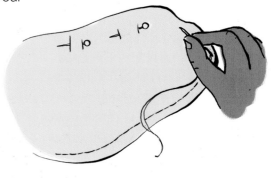

TIP

Why not make a cross-eyed monster? Use a white circle of fabric and sew large stitches across it in a cross shape. And try stitching several layers of fabric on top of each other using running stitch and slipstitch for a really colorful effect!

3 Turn your shape the right way out. Stuff it with Fiberfill, pushing it into any tight corners with the blunt end of a pencil. Thread the needle again. Turn the raw edges along the opening to the inside. Starting and finishing with a few small stitches, sew up the opening with backstitch. Trim the thread.

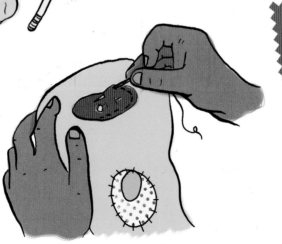

4 Now design a crazy monster face. Cut out shapes from the felt scraps and pin them in position. Cut a length of embroidery floss and thread the needle. Starting with a few stitches to fix the floss in place, sew on the felt shapes with running stitch or slipstitch. Sew on buttons for eyes.

Make a monster **FRIEND TO CUDDLE** in bed!

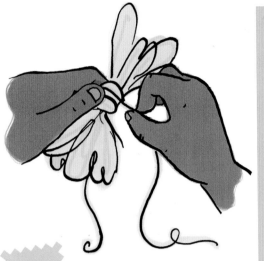

5 To give your monster wild hair, wind some yarn around your hand five or six times. Pull it off and wind another length of yarn around the middle and tie a knot.

6 Thread the large-eyed needle with some more yarn and then stitch the hair onto the monster's head with a few stitches over and over the middle of the hair. Finish with a knot.

Sock monsters

Make a crowd of crazy monsters with all your lonely, old, odd socks, which never have partners. Perhaps they can be friends with any T-shirt creatures you have made (see page 18), but take care—being monsters, they might not get along with each other!

Where do all the ODD SOCKS go?

In this project, you will use:

Running stitch (see page 115)

Sewing on buttons (see page 116)

You will need:

An odd sock (ask an adult first)

Scissors

Yarn (wool) and a needle with a large eye

Fiberfill (stuffing)

Scraps of felt

A needle and thread

Buttons

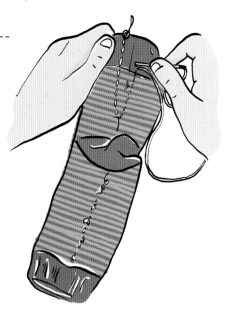

1

To make a monster with ears, turn the sock inside out. Cut a length of yarn and tie a knot at one end. Thread the large needle and sew running stitch from the toe of the sock along for about 2 inches (5 cm) and then back to the toe, leaving a ½-inch (1-cm) gap between the lines of stitching. Finish with a knot and trim the yarn.

2 Cut the sock between the stitch lines, making sure you don't cut into the stitching. Turn the sock the right way out and push the ears out with the wrong end of a pencil.

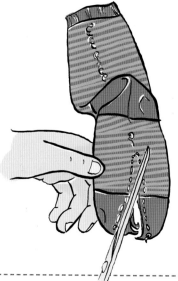

3 Fill the sock with Fiberfill, using small pieces and pushing it into the ears with the pencil. Cut some more yarn and tie a knot at one end. Turn in the end of the sock and sew across it with running stitch. Finish with another knot and trim the yarn.

4 To make a funny mouth, squash the heel part of the sock slightly so that it looks like lips. Sew running stitch along it with yarn, starting and finishing with a knot, then trim the yarn. Finally, sew buttons onto your monster to make eyes.

TIP

What about trying these other monster ideas, too? Use scraps of felt for eyes and mouths. Have some monsters with ears and some without. Have one-eyed monsters and many-eyed monsters. Make some monsters glum and some happy!

Felt mouse

A mouse in a house is fun to make and fun to play with. When you've made your mouse or even a family of mice, make a house with a shoebox and scraps of fabric. Make a toadstool (see page 27) to give the house a lovely woodland look.

In this project, you will use:

Slipstitch (see page 117)

French knot (see page 118)

Running stitch (see page 115)

Using a pattern (see page 114)

Gathering (see page 117)

You will need:

Paper and a pencil

Scissors

Gray and pink felt

Pins

A needle and thread

Fiberfill (stuffing)

A teaspoon

Large dried lentils

Embroidery floss (thread) and a needle

Scraps of fabric for the dress

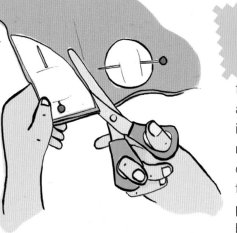

1 Trace the templates on page 123 onto paper, and cut out patterns for the mouse body, the base, and the ears. Fold the gray felt in half and pin the pattern for the mouse body onto it, placing the dotted fold line of the pattern on the fold of the felt. Cut around the pattern. Pin the pattern for the base onto the gray felt (unfolded) and cut it out. Remove all the pins and the patterns.

2 Cut a length of thread, and thread the needle. Fold the mouse body in half. Start with a few small stitches and then sew the long edges together with slipstitch. Keep the stitches quite close together so that the dried lentils you will use for stuffing can't escape. Leave the bottom of the felt open. Finish with a few small stitches.

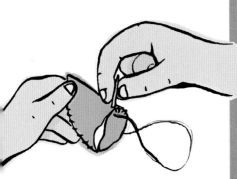

3 Starting with a few small stitches, sew the felt base onto the body with slipstitch, keeping the stitches close together. Leave a gap of about 1 inch (2.5 cm) to push in the Fiberfill.

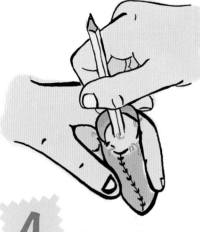

4 Stuff small pieces of Fiberfill into the mouse, pushing it well down into the nose with a pencil.

5 When the mouse is three-quarters full, spoon in some lentils to fill the rest of the space. Hold the mouse carefully upright so that you don't spill the lentils, and stitch up the gap with slipstitch, finishing with a few small stitches. Trim the thread. The lentils are heavy and will make the mouse stand up better.

6

Now for the eyes. Cut a length of embroidery floss and tie a knot at one end. Thread the needle. You don't want ends of floss dangling from the mouse's face, so start at the back of the mouse's head and push the needle through your slipstitches to the mouse's face, so that it comes out in the right place for one of the eyes. Sew a French knot for the eye.

Now push the needle through the mouse's head to the place for the second eye and sew another French knot, then push the needle back through to the back of the head and finish with a small knot. Trim the floss.

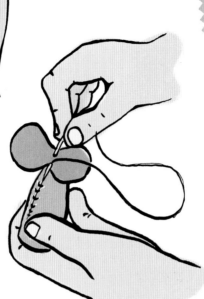

7

Pin the pattern for the ears onto the pink felt. Cut them out. Remove the pins and pattern. Using the needle and thread, sew a few small stitches on the back of the head, then stitch through the ears and then back through the mouse. Repeat this a few times to hold the ears in place and finish with a few small stitches. Trim the thread.

GOOD MORNING Mrs Mouse!

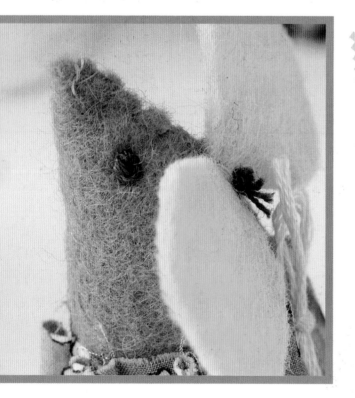

8

To make the dress, cut out a small rectangle of fabric measuring about 5 x 1½ inches (13 x 4 cm). Thread a needle with embroidery floss and stitch along one of the long sides using running stitch. Leave both ends of the floss long. Unthread the needle and tie the dress onto the mouse, with a bow, gathering the dress up around the mouse's neck. Trim the ends of the floss if they are too long.

Felt toadstool

Make a magic toadstool to go with your mouse house (see page 24)—it will add to the woodland look. Like the mouse, the toadstool stalk is partly filled with dried lentils to help it to stand up straight.

In this project, you will use:

Slipstitch (see page 117)

Using a pattern (see page 114)

You will need:

Paper and a pencil

Scissors

Red and white felt

Pins

A needle and white thread

Fiberfill (stuffing)

A teaspoon

Large dried lentils

1 Trace the templates on page 122 onto paper and cut out patterns for the toadstool top, the stalk, and the base. Pin the pattern for the toadstool top onto a piece of red felt and cut around it. Then pin it to a piece of white felt and cut around it again. Pin the stalk and base patterns onto white felt and cut one of each. Remove all the pins and patterns.

2 On scraps of white felt, draw around a small coin or button to make spots for the toadstool. Thread the needle with white thread. On the red felt, start with a few small stitches on the underside of where you want your first spot to be. Then push the needle through to the top and sew on the first spot using slipstitch. When you reach the end of the first spot, push the needle through to the underside again and then back up to the top where you want the next spot to be. Keep going until all the spots have been sewn on. Finish with a few small stitches on the underside and trim the thread.

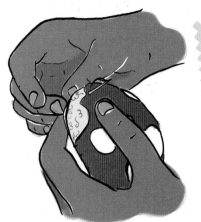

3 Pin the red spotty top to the white felt top. Thread the needle again. Starting with a few small stitches, slipstitch the two parts together around the edge. Leave a small opening of about 1¼ inches (3 cm) and stuff with small pieces of Fiberfill, using the wrong end of the pencil to push it in. Stitch up the opening and finish with a few small stitches. Trim the thread and remove the pins.

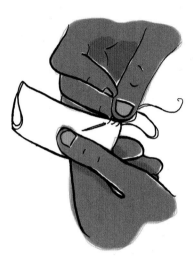

4 Take the felt stalk piece and fold it in half lengthwise. Starting and finishing with a few small stitches, sew the two long edges together with slipstitch. Keep the stitches quite close together so that the dried lentils you will use for stuffing can't escape.

5 Find the circle pattern for the base of the stalk. Place it in the middle of the white base of the toadstool top and draw around it. This is a guide for where to sew on the stalk.

A MAGIC TOADSTOOL for your mouse house!

6 Push the stalk out so that it looks like a tube. Starting with a few small stitches just inside the circle you have drawn, use slipstitch to sew one end of the tube to the underside of the toadstool top. Stitch onto the pencil circle. Finish with a few small stitches. Trim the thread.

7 Push some Fiberfill inside the stalk, filling it about halfway up. Now, starting with a few small stitches, begin to stitch the base onto the open end of the stalk with slipstitch. Halfway around, spoon dried lentils into the stalk until it is full. Holding the stalk carefully upright so that the lentils don't spill, finish sewing the base onto the stalk. End with a few small stitches. Finally, trim the thread.

Add the toadstool to your mouse house!

Felt cupcakes

Tease your friends with these yummy-looking felt cakes or use them in a play-shop or for a teddy bear's picnic. Choose felt in pretty pastel colors finished with a red cherry or, for chocolate cakes, use brown felt, adding some rickrack trim for a delicious cream filling!

1 Trace the templates on page 123 onto paper and cut out the patterns for the cupcake top, the cupcake bottom, the frosting (icing), and the cherry. Pin the large circle onto felt in a pastel shade, the medium-sized circle onto brown or beige felt, and the frosting shape onto white or pastel-colored felt. Cut out. Remove the pins and patterns.

In this project, you will use:

Running stitch (see page 115)

Using a pattern (see page 114)

You will need:

Paper and a pencil

Scissors

Pins

A selection of felt in browns, pastel shades, and red for the cherry

Embroidery floss (thread) in similar colors to the felts

A needle

Fiberfill (stuffing)

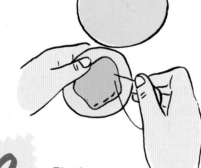

2 Pin the frosting shape onto the cupcake top shape. Cut a length of embroidery floss and tie a knot at one end. Thread the needle. Starting from the back of the felt, sew running stitch all the way around the frosting to hold the two pieces together. Finish with another knot on the back of the felt. Remove the pins.

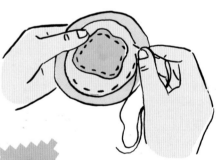

3 Put these joined pieces of felt in the middle of the largest felt circle. Knot the floss and sew running stitch around the edge of the cupcake top, as you did in Step 2, making the stitches quite big. Leave a gap of about 1 inch (2.5 cm) for the Fiberfill.

These fun cupcakes look GOOD ENOUGH TO EAT!

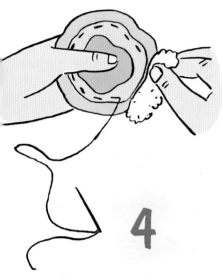

4

Take small pieces of the Fiberfill and carefully push them inside the cupcake through the gap. Add enough to make the cupcake nicely rounded. When you have finished stuffing the cupcake, continue the running stitch to close the gap and finish with a knot on the underside.

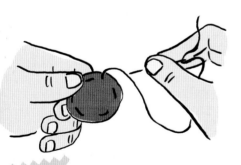

5

Pin the paper pattern for the cherry to the red felt and cut it out. Remove the pins and pattern. Cut a length of floss, tie a knot at one end, and thread the needle. Sew running stitch around the outside of the felt.

6

Pull the floss slightly to gather the cherry up. Stuff it with a small piece of fiberfill. Pull the floss a little more and sew a few stitches to hold it in place. Don't cut the floss. Stitch the cherry to the top of the cup cake using a few small stitches and finish with a knot or several little stitches to hold it in place. Trim the floss.

Cowboy horse

Let's gallop! A big stuffed sock and a broomstick make a horse for a cowboy or a pony for a show jumper! Sew strips of fabric for the mane and add buttons for eyes.

In this project, you will use:

Running stitch (see page 115)

Sewing on buttons (see page 116)

Using a pattern (see page 114)

You will need:

A big, old, adult sock (ask before you take one!)

Fiberfill (stuffing)

An elastic band

Scissors

Pieces of fabric in different colors

Yarn (wool) and a needle with a large eye

Paper and a pencil

Pins

Felt for the ears

2 buttons

Craft glue and spreader

A broom handle

1 Stuff the sock with Fiberfill to make the horse's head. Pull off small pieces and push it in evenly to make sure that there are no lumps and bumps. Don't fill it too full. Close up the end with an elastic band.

2 To make your horse's mane, tear strips of fabric about 1 inch (2–3 cm) wide. To tear fabric, make a small snip at one side and then rip it apart—it will rip in a straight line. Cut the strips into lengths about 6 inches (15 cm) long.

3 Thread a length of yarn through the large needle. Tie a knot in the yarn. Starting at the back of the sock (near the closed-up top), stitch through the sock and then through the first strip, then back into the sock and up through the next strip. Make stitches through the middle of the strips all the way up the back of the sock toward where the horse's ears will be. Finish with a knot and trim the yarn.

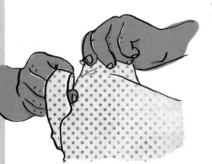

4 Trace the template on page 120 onto paper and cut out a pattern for the horse's ears. Fold the felt in half and pin the pattern onto it. Cut around the pattern to give you two ears. Remove the pins and pattern.

Now thread and knot another piece of yarn. Sew one ear into position on the horse's head with running stitch. Finish with a knot. Sew on the other ear in the same way.

5 Thread and knot another piece of yarn and sew on the two buttons for the eyes.

6 Spread glue onto one end of the broom handle where the sock will cover it. Now push the broom handle carefully inside the horse's head through the elastic band, which will hold the sock tightly in place onto the glue. Cut a long piece of yarn and fold it double. Wind it tightly around the elastic band and then tie it with a double knot and then a bow, so that the head will be even more secure.

Rag dolls

Why not make one of these adorable dolls? This is a really lovely project and it's not difficult, but it will take a bit longer to finish than some of the others. Once you've made a doll, why not make some clothes (see pages 38—41) for her, too?

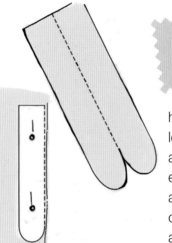

In this project, you will use:

Slipstitch (see page 117)

Using a pattern (see page 114)

You will need:

Paper and a pencil

Scissors

Two 8½ x 11-inch (A4) pieces of felt in flesh color for the body, arms, and legs

One 8½ x 11-inch (A4) piece of felt in a different color for the hair

Pins

Needle and embroidery floss (thread) in the same colors as the two felts

Fiberfill (stuffing)

Scraps of felt for the eyes and mouth

Craft glue

Gingham ribbon for the bow

1 Photocopy the templates on page 126 at double the size, then cut out paper patterns for the body, an arm, a leg, and the front and back of the hair. Put the patterns for the hair to one side. The patterns for the arm and leg must be pinned so the dotted edge is on a fold of felt. Fold over just enough felt to pin them on, and cut around them. Do not cut the fold! Remove the pins and patterns. You need two arms and two legs, so do this again on another fold.

Then fold the felt again, pin on the pattern for the body and cut out two body pieces.

2

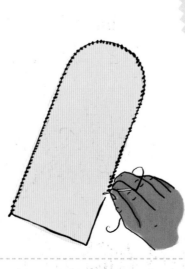

Pin the two body pieces together. Cut a length of flesh-colored embroidery floss and tie a knot at one end. Thread the needle. Starting at a bottom corner of the body, use slipstitch to sew all the way around the edge to the other corner, leaving the bottom edge open. Finish with a knot and trim the floss. Remove the pins. Put the body to one side.

3

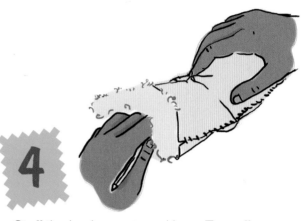

Take a leg piece and fold it in half lengthwise. Pin to hold it in place. Starting and finishing with a knot, slipstitch around the foot and down the leg, leaving the top open. Remove the pins. Sew both legs in this way, then do the same for both arms.

4

Stuff the body, arms, and legs. Tear off small pieces of Fiberfill and push it down to the ends first. Use the blunt end of a pencil to help you. Don't stuff them too tightly— leave a little space to sew them up.

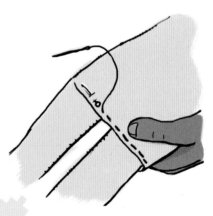

5

Push the tops of the legs inside the bottom edge of the body and pin in place. Cut a length of floss and tie a knot at one end. Push the needle through from the back of the doll and sew running stitch all the way across the bottom, finishing with a knot on the back. Remove the pins.

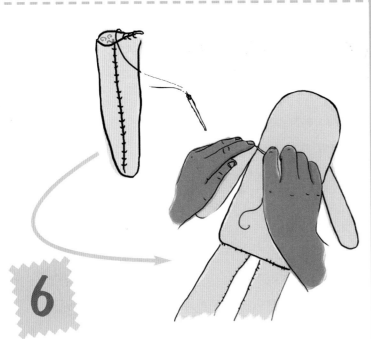

6

Take the arms and slipstitch across the top, with the seam in the middle. Start and finish with a knot in the floss. Slipstitch the arms in place on the body with the seam underneath, starting and finishing with a knot.

7

Pin the two hair patterns from Step 1 onto the hair-colored felt and cut them out. Cut a length of hair-colored embroidery floss and tie a knot at one end. Thread the needle. Starting and finishing with a knot, slipstitch the two hair pieces together.

Place the hair on the doll's head and stitch it on with a few small stitches through the hair, into the top of the head and out again. Next, use scraps of colored felt to cut out small dots for eyes and a smiley mouth. Glue them onto the doll's face with a dab of craft glue. Add a bow or pretty flower if you like, either sewing it in place or using another small dab of glue. Finally, tie a gingham ribbon around the doll's neck.

Now all she needs are some clothes!

Doll's clothes

Once you have sewn your rag doll (see page 34), you will need to dress her. Make a pretty skirt and top, and a stylish coat, then finish with a cute pair of shoes. Of course, you could make clothes like these for any doll, although you might have to change the sizes.

In this project, you will use:

Running stitch (see page 115)

Slipstitch (see page 117)

Sewing on buttons (see page 116)

Using a pattern (see page 114)

You will need:

Squared paper, a pencil, and a ruler

Fabric for the top

Pinking shears

Pins

A needle and thread

Scissors

Braid or rickrack (optional)

A small piece of touch-and-close tape (Velcro)

Fabric for the skirt

A safety pin

Ribbon for the skirt, about 12 inches (30 cm) long

17 x 11-inch (A3) piece of felt for the coat

Felt for the shoes

2 buttons

Small scissors

1

For the top: Draw a rectangle measuring 5 x 10¼ inches (13 x 26 cm) on the squared paper and cut it out. Pin it to the fabric and cut around it with pinking shears. Fold over the two short edges to the wrong side by about ½ inch (1 cm). Pin in place. Thread the needle and, starting with a few small stitches, sew running stitch along each fold. Finish with a more few small stitches to hold the thread in place. Trim the thread. Remove the pins.

2

Fold over the top edge of the fabric to the wrong side by about ½ inch (1 cm). Pin in place and, starting and finishing with a few small stitches, sew running stitch along this fold. If you wish, sew braid or rickrack along it using running stitch. Trim the thread and remove the pins.

 Separate the touch-and-close tape and sew one piece to the right side of the fabric, in the top left-hand corner, using small running stitches. Start on the wrong side with a knot in the thread, stitch around all four sides of the tape, and finish with another knot on the wrong side.

In the same way, stitch the other half of the tape to the wrong side of the fabric, in the top right-hand corner, so that when the two sides of the top overlap the tape pieces will stick together. Wrap the top around the doll and fasten at the back with the tape.

4 **For the skirt**:
Draw a rectangle measuring 21 x 7½ inches (54 x 19 cm) on the squared paper and cut it out. Pin it to the fabric and cut around it with pinking shears. Fold over the two short edges to the wrong side by about ½ inch (1 cm) and sew running stitch along them, as in Step 1.

 Fold over the top edge of the fabric by about ¾ inch (2 cm) and sew running stitch along it, keeping the stitching about ½ inch (1 cm) away from the fold to make a channel for the ribbon.

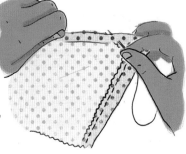

Tie the ribbon around the doll's waist and fasten with a bow at the back.

6 Fasten the safety pin through one end of the ribbon. Thread the safety pin and ribbon through the channel at the top of the rectangle.

8 **For the coat**: Photocopy the template on page 126 at double the size and cut out a paper pattern for the jacket. Fold the felt in half. Pin the pattern onto the felt, positioning the dotted line of the shoulders along the fold. When you cut around it, this will give you the front and back of the coat, joined at the shoulders. Cut around the pattern. Cut out the neck circle, but do not cut along the shoulder folds.

You will need to cut open the front of the jacket. To do this, use a pencil to draw a dot on the felt at the top and bottom of the center line, which is shown on the pattern. Remove the pins and pattern. Join the two dots with a ruler and pencil. Open out the jacket and cut along the line.

9 Fold the jacket along the shoulders again and pin it together under the arms and along the sides. Thread the needle and slipstitch the two sides together, starting and finishing with a few small stitches. Trim the thread. Remove the pins.

STYLISH CLOTHES for a special doll!

10 Fold back a little of the felt around the neck to make a collar. Sew a few small stitches in the corners of the collar to hold them in place. Trim the thread. Sew on buttons for decoration.

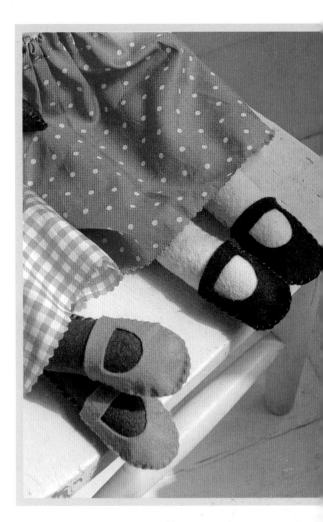

11 **For the shoes**: Photocopy the templates on page 126 at double the size and cut out paper patterns for the front and back of the shoes. Using small sharp scissors, cut out the peephole in the pattern for the front of the shoes. Fold the felt in half, pin on the patterns, and cut around them so you have two backs and two fronts. Remove the pins and pattern from the backs.

12 On each of the shoe fronts, use a pencil to draw around the peepholes in the pattern onto the felt. Use the small scissors to cut out the holes. Pin each top piece of felt to a bottom piece and slipstitch around the edges, leaving the tops open. Start and finish with a few small stitches to hold the thread in place. Trim the thread. Remove the pins.

Dress your doll in her gorgeous new clothes!

CHAPTER TWO

Fashion fun

Button badges

In this project you can go wild with your color choices; in fact, the brighter the better! Show off your sewing skills with gorgeous embroidery and sew on pretty shaped buttons to create cute badges or hair clips—fun decorations that cost practically nothing to make.

Colorful badges to SHOW OFF YOUR SEWING SKILLS!

In this project, you could use (but you don't have to use all of them!):

French knot (see page 118)

Backstitch (see page 115)

Straight stitch (see page 119)

Chain and fly stitch (see page 119)

Seed stitch (see page 119)

Daisy stitch (see page 119)

Sewing on buttons (see page 116)

You will need:

Paper and a pencil

Craft glue (if you are using thin felt)

Small pieces of thick or thin felt in bright colors

A fade-away marker pen

Embroidery floss (thread) in bright colors

Buttons in pretty shapes

Safety pins and/or hair clips

1 Trace the templates on page 120 onto paper, and cut out the patterns. If you have thick felt, pin each pattern to the felt and cut around it. If you only have thin felt, cut out two identical shapes for each badge and glue them together with a little craft glue. Draw the stitch design on the felt shapes with a fade-away marker pen (or you could design your own patterns).

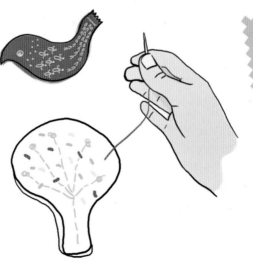

2 Using the stitch key on page 120, embroider the patterns in brightly colored embroidery floss, always starting and finishing with a knot at the back of the badge.

3 Sew on buttons to decorate the badges.

4 Sew safety pins to the back of the shapes you want as badges. Sew simple hair clips to the ones you want as hair decorations. As you sew, make sure that the needle does not go through to the front of the badge, as the stitching will show.

Pin them to your favorite jacket!

Christmas book bag

You could make this special Christmas bag as a gift for your best friend or for a member of your family—or why not make it just for you? That way, your favorite Christmas books will never go missing!

NEVER LOSE your favorite BOOK!

In this project, you will use:

Running stitch (see page 115)

Slipstitch (see page 117)

You will need:

A large piece of paper and pencil

A ruler

12 inches (30 cm) wool fabric, 44 inches (112 cm) wide

Pinking shears

A needle

White yarn (wool)

26 inches (66 cm) silver rickrack

Scissors

Craft glue

Scraps of decorated white felt for pot and ball

1 Draw a rectangle 22 x 10 inches (56 x 25 cm) on a large piece of paper (or newspaper) and cut it out. Pin this pattern to the wool fabric and cut around it with pinking shears. Fold over both the short ends by ½ inch (1 cm) and pin them in place. Cut a length of white yarn and tie a knot in it. Sew along one of the folds in running stitch, using quite big stitches—about ½ inch (1 cm) long.

2 When you have finished, turn the fabric round and stitch back over the stitches you have just sewn, pushing the needle in where it came out before and pulling it out where it went in before. This will fill in all the gaps between the stitches. Finish with a knot. Repeat at the other end of the bag.

Then ask an adult to help you press the hems flat, using a warm iron.

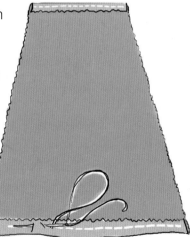

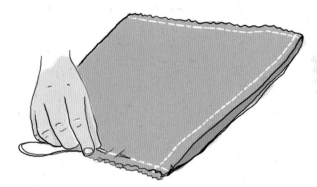

3 Fold the piece of fabric in half widthwise with wrong sides together (the two hems you have just stitched will be inside the bag) and pin in place. Stitch along the two side edges, first in running stitch one way and then coming back in running stitch the other way, filling in the gaps, just as you did for the two hems.

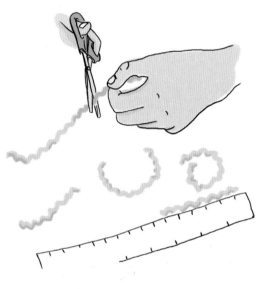

4 Using a ruler, carefully cut nine lengths of silver rickrack to the following measurements: 6 inches, 5 inches, 4 inches, 3 inches, 2½ inches, 2 inches, 1½ inches, 1 inch, ½ inch (15 cm, 13 cm, 10 cm, 7 cm, 6 cm, 5 cm, 3.5 cm, 2.5 cm, 1 cm). Cut the ends on the diagonal to stop them fraying.

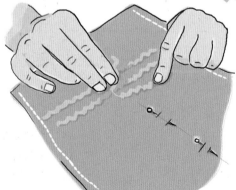

5 To help you glue the rickrack in the right position, fold the bag in half to find the center. Mark the center line with a line of pins.

Now start with the longest piece of rickrack. First, fold it in half to make a clear crease. Then lay it face down on some newspaper, with something heavy at each end to hold it flat.

Carefully trickle a very thin line of glue along the back and then lay it on the bag about 3 inches (7 cm) up from the bottom with the center crease on your line of pins—it doesn't matter if you glue over a pin. Press it flat using your fingers. Do the same with the next longest piece, gluing it about ¾ inch (2 cm) above the first piece and keeping the center crease on the line of pins.

Keep doing this with all the pieces, working from longest to shortest to make a Christmas tree shape. Remove all the pins.

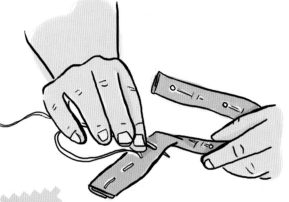

6 Draw a pot shape on paper and cut it out. Make sure it is the right size and shape for your Christmas tree and then draw around it on the felt. Draw around a coin to make the decoration for the top of the tree. Cut them out and glue them in place.

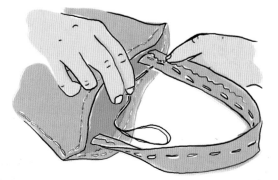

7 To make the handles, first draw a rectangle measuring 13 x 2½ inches (33 x 6 cm) on paper. Fold the fabric in half, pin the pattern onto the folded fabric, and cut around it to give you two long strips.

Ask an adult to help you with the next stage. Fold over one of the long edges by ¾ inch (2 cm) and press it flat with a warm iron. Now fold the other long edge over the top of this by ½ inch (1 cm) and press that flat. Do the same for the other handle. Then, starting and finishing with a knot, stitch along the center of each handle using running stitch.

8 Pin the end of one handle to the inside of the bag about 2 inches (5 cm) from the side seam and overlapping the top of the bag by about 1¼ inches (4 cm). Being careful not to twist the handle, pin the other end to the bag about 2 inches (5 cm) from the other side seam.

Starting and finishing with a knot, stitch neatly around both ends of the handle using slipstitch. Now sew on the other handle in the same way.

Hair barrettes

These gorgeous hair barrettes are very quick to make and are a great way of using up scraps of felt left over from other projects. Make one to go with a special outfit, or why not give one as a birthday present to your sister or a friend?

1 Trace the templates on page 121 onto paper and cut out a circle or heart shape. Fold the felt and pin the pattern onto it. Cut around the pattern. This will give you two shapes. Remove the pins and pattern. Pin the shapes together.

In this project, you will use:

Blanket stitch (see page 116)

Sewing on buttons (see page 116)

Using a pattern (see page 114)

You will need:

Paper and a pencil

Scissors

Felt

Pins

Embroidery floss and a needle

Fiberfill (stuffing)

A button

Metal barrettes (hair slides)

2 Cut a length of embroidery floss and tie a knot at one end. Thread the needle. Sew blanket stitch around the felt, leaving a small opening.

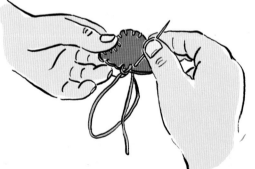

3 Stuff the shape with little pieces of Fiberfill.

4 Continue using blanket stitch to close the opening and finish with a knot at the back of the shape. Trim the floss.

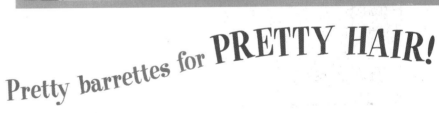

Pretty barrettes for **PRETTY HAIR!**

5 Sew a button onto the front of the shape.

6 Thread the needle with another piece of embroidery floss and tie a knot at the end. Make a stitch through the back of the shape and then stitch through the barrette. Stitch through the back of the shape and the barrette about four more times so that they are held firmly together. Finish with a knot and trim the floss.

Flower hair tie

Brighten up your braid or ponytail with this cute hair decoration. Make a felt flower with a button in the center and sew it onto a hair elastic. It is quick and easy to make from small scraps of felt, so why not make a pair for when you have two braids?

In this project, you will use:

Using a pattern (see page 114)

You will need:

Paper and a pencil

Scissors

Pins

Felt in 2 colors for the flower and in green for the leaves

Embroidery floss (thread) and a needle

Pretty button

An elastic hair tie

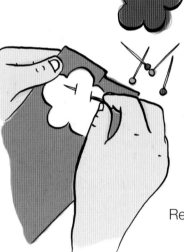

1 Trace the templates on page 121 onto paper and cut out patterns for the flower and the leaf. Pin the flower shape onto one of the pieces of felt and cut around it. Remove the pin and pattern. Pin the pattern onto a different color of felt and cut out another flower. Remove the pins and pattern.

2 Fold the green felt in half. Pin the leaf pattern onto it and cut it out. Remove the pins and pattern to give you two leaf shapes.

Pretty flowers for PRETTY HAIRSTYLES!

3

Put the two flower shapes on top of one another, and place the leaf shapes behind them. Cut a length of embroidery floss. Thread the needle and tie a knot at one end. Starting at the back, stitch through the two leaves (near their ends) and through the center of the flowers. Pull the floss so that the knot is tight against the felt.

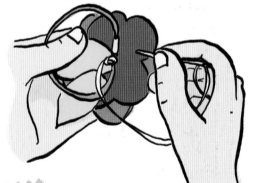

4

Take the button and push the needle through one of the buttonholes. Pull the button along the floss so that it sits in the middle of the flower.

5

Stitch back through the other hole in the button and push the needle carefully back though all the layers of felt. Repeat this stitch up through the felt and the button and back down again to hold all the layers firmly together. If you are using a button with four holes, then make two more stitches through the other holes, as well.

Stitch a couple of small stitches through the back leaf only to hold everything firmly together. Leave your needle threaded.

6

Now stitch the hair tie onto the back of the flower and leaves with four or five stitches looped over the elastic. Finish with a knot. Easy!

Drawstring bag

This little bag is very easy to make and is perfect for storing toys, jewelry, and little treasures. You could also make one as a gift for a friend or someone in your family, filling it with candy, pretty shells, or beads.

Tiny treasure bags for SPECIAL BITS and pieces!

In this project, you will use:

Running stitch (see page 115)

Backstitch (see page 115)

You will need:

Fabric

A large book or magazine

Pinking shears

A ruler

A pencil

Scissors

A needle and thread

A large safety pin

Narrow ribbon (less than ¾ inch/2 cm wide)

Scraps of felt

Embroidery floss (thread) and a needle

1 Draw a rectangle measuring about 14 x 10 inches (35 x 25 cm) on the wrong side of the fabric. It doesn't really matter exactly what size the rectangle is, so simply draw around a large book or magazine.

Cut out the rectangle with pinking shears, which will help to stop the fabric fraying. Lay the rectangle of fabric on the table, with the wrong side facing up and with a long edge at the top. Measure 1½ inches (4 cm) down from both top corners and make a mark with the pencil. Using scissors, make a snip about ½ inch (1 cm) long on both sides at this point.

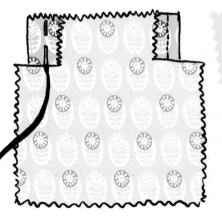

2 Fold over the flap of fabric above one snip and pin it in place. Cut a length of thread and thread the needle. Starting and finishing with a few small stitches, sew running stitch along the flap to hold it in place. Do the same with the other flap. Remove the pins.

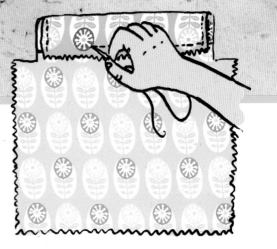

 3 Fold the top edge of the fabric rectangle down over the flaps you have just sewn down. Pin it. The fold will be about ¾ inch (2 cm) wide and the flaps you have sewn down will be inside this fold. Starting and finishing with a few small stitches, sew backstitch along the bottom of the fold. Remove the pins. This will be the top of the bag and the ribbon tie will be threaded through it.

4

With right sides together, fold the fabric in half lining up the edges. Pin together, then sew backstitch down the side and along the bottom to form a bag. Start and finish with a few small stitches as before. Turn the bag the right way out.

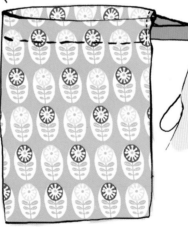

5

Cut a piece of ribbon about 18 inches (45 cm) long. Fasten the safety pin through one end of the ribbon and push it through the channel at the top of the bag, gathering up the fabric, until it comes out of the other side.

6

Remove the safety pin and stitch the two ends of the ribbon together with a few small stitches.

7

Finally, find something small and round to draw around. Draw and cut out two circles of felt and pin them together, with the ribbon ends inside them. Using embroidery floss, sew them together with a small running stitch around the edge. Make sure that one stitch goes through the ribbon so that the ribbon won't pull out. Finish with a few small stitches. Trim the floss.

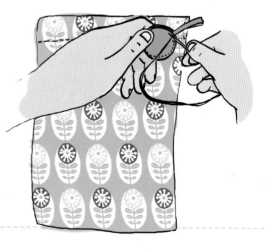

Cat bag

You can't take all cats for a walk, but you can take this one! It's perfect for carrying all your bits and pieces. This is an easy project with easy fabric—fleece is great to use, because it doesn't fray.

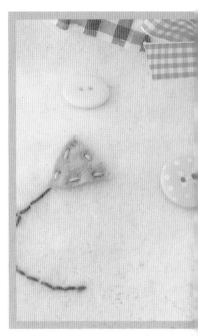

In this project, you will use:

Running stitch (see page 115)

Backstitch (see page 115)

Sewing on buttons (see page 116)

Using a pattern (see page 114)

You will need:

Paper and a pencil

Scissors

9 x 18 inches (23 x 46 cm) fleece fabric

Pins

Embroidery floss (thread) in 2 colors and a needle

Felt for the nose

A scrap of colored fabric for the ears

2 buttons

Wide ribbon for the handle

Narrow ribbon for the bow

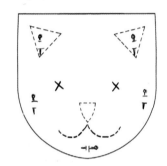

 1 Photocopy the template on page 125 at double the size, then cut out patterns for the bag, nose, and ears. Fold the fleece fabric in half and pin the bag pattern to it. Cut around the pattern. Remove the pins and pattern. You will have two bag shapes.

2 Take one of the bag shapes and, using the template as a guide, mark on it the positions of the eyes, nose, mouth, and ears.

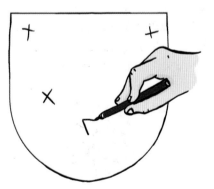

Where are you off to, PUSSYCAT?

3

Pin the pattern for the nose onto the felt and cut around it. Remove the pins and pattern. Choose one color of embroidery for stitching on the cat's face. Cut a length of this embroidery floss and tie a knot at one end. Thread the needle. Starting with a knot on the back of the fleece, sew the felt nose in place using running stitch. Finish with a knot on the back and trim the floss.

Embroider a mouth shape in backstitch with the same color of floss, starting and finishing with a knot on the back of the fleece. Trim the floss.

4

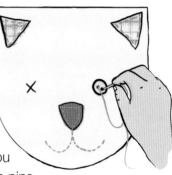

Fold the scrap of colored fabric in half and pin on the pattern for the ear. Cut around it so you have two ears. Remove the pins and pattern.

Pin the ears in place and, starting and finishing with a knot inside the bag, sew on the ears with running stitch. Remove the pins. Sew buttons in place for the eyes.

6

Turn the bag the right way out. Fold over the top edge of the bag to the inside by about ½ inch (1 cm) and pin in place. Cut a length of the second color of embroidery floss and tie a knot in it.

Starting from the inside of the bag, sew running stitch all the way around the top of the bag. Remove the pins as you sew. Finish with a knot inside the bag. Trim the floss.

5

Now pin the two sides of the bag together with right sides facing (the cat face will be inside).

Use the other color of embroidery floss for sewing the bag together. Cut a length of this embroidery floss and tie a knot at one end. Thread the needle. Sew backstitch all the way around the curved edge, leaving the top open. Finish with a knot, and trim the floss. Remove the pins.

7 Take another piece of the second color of embroidery floss and tie a knot at one end. Starting from the inside of the bag, sew running stitch around the curve of the bag. These stitches are part of the decoration, so try to keep them neat and even. Finish with a knot inside the bag. Trim the floss.

Put it over your shoulder and off you go to the shops!

8 For the handle, cut a 39-inch (100-cm) length of wide ribbon. Sew one end to one side of the bag with a few stitches then, taking care not to twist the ribbon, sew the other end to the other side of the bag.

Finally, make a ribbon bow and sew it onto the bag by first making a few stitches in the bag and then sewing through the back of the ribbon a few times. Finish with a few small stitches inside the bag.

Felted bag

Felt is a really easy fabric to use, as it doesn't need hemming. To make your own felt, put an old wool sweater (check with an adult first!) in a washing machine at a temperature of about 160°F (70°C) and, hey presto, when the sweater dries it will have shrunk and become felted, ready for you to turn into something else.

In this project, you will use:

Slipstitch (see page 117)

Sewing on buttons (see page 116)

Using a pattern (see page 114)

You will need:

A woolen sweater

Washing machine (ask an adult to help you use it)

Scissors

A large button

Yarn (wool) and a needle with a large eye

Paper and a pencil

A needle and thread

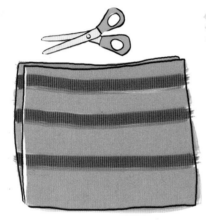

1

Wash the sweater in the washing machine at 160°F (70°C) to felt it. Let it dry, then cut out a rectangle measuring 8 x 9½ inches (20 x 24 cm). The easiest way to do this is to find a book that is about this size and draw around it. Fold the rectangle in half.

2

Thread a length of yarn through the large needle. Tie a knot in the yarn. Stitch along one side of the bag using slipstitch. Finish with a knot. Now do the other side.

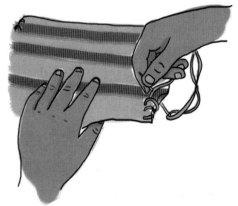

3

Cut 2 straps from the sweater. You can use the ribbing at the bottom of the sweater for a different texture of felt. Make the straps about 1 inch (2.5 cm) wide and about 8 inches (20 cm) long.

4

Stitch each end onto the bag with four big stitches.

5

Trace the template on page 121 onto paper and cut out a pattern for the flower. Pin it onto the felted wool and cut around it. Cut out two flower shapes. You could cut one from the ribbing and one from another part of the sweater to give different textures or colors.

6

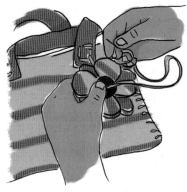

Thread another length of yarn through the large needle and tie a knot in it. Lay one flower on top of the other and stitch through both flowers and then up through the button and back down through the button and both flowers. Stitch two or three stitches like this and finish at the back of the flowers with a knot.

Then use the needle and thread to sew the flower to the bag. Start with a few small stitches on the bag, then sew through the back of the flower. Sew a few more stitches through both layers and finish with a few small stitches.

Cardigan pencil case

Recycle an old cardigan into a cool pencil case. It will be unique, because you've made it yourself! Check with an adult before you use your old cardigan, though. You can add your initials so it won't get lost at school.

In this project, you will use:

Backstitch (see page 115)

Slipstitch (see page 117)

Sewing on buttons (see page 116)

You will need:

An old cardigan with button fastenings (ask an adult before you cut one up!)

A pencil

A ruler

Squared paper (for example, from a math book)

Scissors

Pins

Embroidery floss (thread) and needle

Scraps of felt

A pen

1 Using a pencil and ruler, draw a 6 x 10-inch (15 x 26-cm) rectangle on squared paper. Cut it out to make a paper pattern.

Do the cardigan buttons up, turn the cardigan inside out, and lay it flat on the table, button side up. Lay the pattern on the cardigan with the buttons about 2 inches (5 cm) from one long edge of the rectangle. Pin the pattern down.

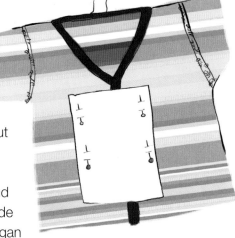

2 Cut around the pattern, making sure you cut through both layers of the cardigan. Remove the pins and pattern. Pin again to hold the two layers together.

Impress your **FRIENDS** *at school with your new pencil case!*

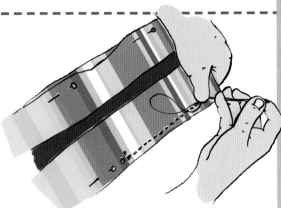

3 Cut a length of embroidery floss and thread the needle. Starting and finishing with a few small stitches, sew around the rectangle using backstitch. Trim the floss.

4 Undo the buttons and turn your pencil case the right way out, pushing out the corners to make a nice rectangle.

5 To add your initials to the case, draw letters on scraps of felt with a pen and cut them out. Pin the letters to the front of the pencil case.

Starting and finishing with a knot on the inside, slipstitch the letters in place with embroidery floss. It's a good idea to put a piece of paper inside the pencil case while sewing on the initials to stop you sewing through both layers of the pencil case. Trim the floss and remove the pins.

6 Sew on extra buttons if there are any missing.

Fill the case with all your pens and pencils!

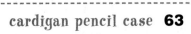

Embroidered jeans

Using simple stitches and sequins, add a flash of color and sparkle to boring, plain jeans to make them perfect for a party or disco. Will you embroider one leg or two? It's up to you!

Pull on your jeans AND PARTY!

In this project, you will use:

Single chain stitch (see page 118)

You will need:

A pair of jeans (ask an adult before embroidering them!)

A fine felt-tip pen (but **not** permanent—check with an adult first if you're not sure), a sharp white coloring pencil, or chalk

Scissors

Embroidery floss (thread) in pretty colors, including green for the leaves, and a needle

Scissors

A needle and thread

Sequins

Bugle beads

1 Mark the position of the flowers at the bottom of one leg of your jeans with the felt-tip pen, white coloring pencil, or chalk. Keep the marks as small as you can. Cut a length of embroidery floss and tie a knot at one end. Thread the needle. Starting from the inside of the legs, push the needle through for the first flower and sew five chain stitches in a flower shape. Finish with a knot inside the leg and trim the floss. Repeat for the other flowers—we have sewn three flowers in three different colors.

2 Cut a length of green embroidery floss and tie a knot at one end. Thread the needle. Starting from the inside of the leg, push the needle through in position for the first leaf. Sew one chain stitch here to look like a leaf and then take the needle back inside the leg and out in the position of the next leaf. Sew three stitches like this. Finish with a knot inside the leg and trim the floss.

3

To add sequins to the flowers, cut a length of thread and thread the needle. Starting from inside the leg, sew a few small stitches close to a flower to fix the thread in place.

Bring the needle up through the denim in the center of the flower, push it through the sequin hole, then back through the denim at the sequin edge. Bring the needle back through the sequin again and back down through the denim on the other side of the sequin. Take the needle up through the center of the next flower and sew on the next sequin, and the next in the same way. Finish with a few small stitches on the inside of the leg. Trim the thread.

If you want to, now embroider the other leg as well!

4

Sew on bugle beads in between the flower petals in the same way as the sequins, stitching through them just once to hold them in place.

CHAPTER THREE

Delightful decorations

Kissing doves

Doves are signs of peace and the heart is a sign of love. You could make this very special decoration as a sign of peace and love. Tie your doves between branches in a vase or to a shelf edge or a Christmas tree with big red bows.

1 Photocopy the templates on page 127 at double the size, then cut out paper patterns for the dove, the heart, and the wing. Fold the gray felt in half. Pin on the dove pattern and cut around it to make two dove shapes. Do this again so you have four dove shapes. Fold the blue felt in half and pin on the wing shape. Cut around it so you have two wing shapes. Then cut out two heart shapes from the red felt in the same way.

2 Lay out two dove shapes so that they are facing each other and mark the position of the eyes. Thread the needle with black thread. Starting on the back of the first dove, sew a few small stitches, then push the needle through to the front and through a black bead. Push the needle to the back again. Make two more stitches through the bead like this and finish with a few small stitches on the back of the dove. Sew the eye on the second dove in the same way.

3 Place the doves facing each other again and lay on the two wing shapes. Pin them in place. Thread the needle with gray thread. Starting with a few small stitches on the back of the first dove, stitch up through the dove, the wing and a button. Stitch on the button and finish with a few small stitches on the back. Do the same for the other dove.

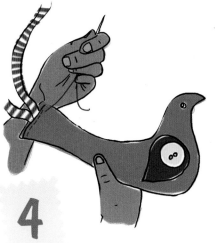

4 Pin a back onto each of the doves. Cut the red ribbon in half. Fold one piece in half to find the center. Pin the center of the ribbon between the two layers of the dove's tail, with the ends hanging free. Now do the same with the other half of the ribbon in the tail of the second dove.

Thread the needle with blue embroidery floss and, starting with a knot, stitch around each dove using running stitch. When you reach the ribbon, make sure that you stitch through both layers of ribbon as well as the felt to secure it. Leave an opening of about 1¼ inches (3 cm) at the bottom of the dove for stuffing.

5 Stuff the doves with small pieces of Fiberfill, using a pencil to push it into the beaks and tails. Stitch up the openings and finish with a few small stitches. Trim the thread and remove the pins.

6 Next, using red floss, sew the two heart pieces together leaving a small gap for stuffing. Stuff with Fiberfill, and stitch the gap closed.

7 Finally, stitch the heart between the doves, using a few small stitches through each dove's beak.

Tree treasures

These blue and white felt decorations—the colors of snow and snow shadows—will look perfect on the Christmas tree! Show off your skills by embroidering them with beautiful patterns. Or why not make a winter wonderland for Christmas by hanging them on frosty white or silver painted twigs, as we've done here?

In this project, you will use:

Backstitch (see page 115)

French knot (see page 118)

Star stitch (see page 119)

You will need:

Paper and a pencil

White felt

Pale blue felt

A fade-away marker pen

Blue, green, and white embroidery floss (thread)

Narrow pale gray satin ribbon (about ¼ inch/5 mm wide)

A needle and white thread

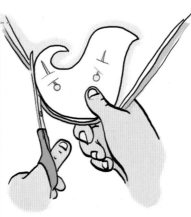

 1 Trace the templates on page 121 onto paper and cut out a pattern for each of the three different tree treasures. Lay the white felt on top of the blue felt and pin on the patterns, pinning through both layers of felt. Cut around each of the three shapes. You will end up with a white front and a blue back for each shape.

2 You can either design your own pattern to embroider onto the shapes or you can use the stitch key on page 121. Use a fade-away marker pen to draw the pattern on the first white felt shape. As the pen lines will fade away quite quickly, don't draw more than one at a time.

Wintery decorations for a WHITE CHRISTMAS

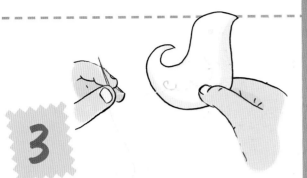

3

Cut a piece of embroidery floss and knot the end. Starting from the back of the white shape, embroider the pattern. Finish with a knot on the back.

Place the white shape up against the matching blue shape to find which side of the blue shape you need to embroider. Draw the embroidery pattern on the blue shape and start stitching again. Finish with a knot on the back. Place the white and the blue sides together, right sides facing outward.

4 To make the ribbon loop, cut an 8-inch (20-cm) length of ribbon. Fold it in half lengthwise and place the ends between the blue and white felt pieces. Pin in place.

Now thread the needle with white thread. Sew a few small stitches on the inside, to hold the thread in place, and then stitch three or four back stitches across the top, making sure that you stitch through both layers of felt and both layers of ribbon. Finish with a few more small stitches on the inside and trim the thread. (For the bird, sew the ribbon just behind the head so that the bird hangs straight.)

5 Now make the other two tree treasures. You'll get quicker with practice!

Hang them on the tree—or find some twigs and get painting!

Barrette holder

Need somewhere to store all your hair accessories? This cute holder is the perfect thing! Your barrettes slide over the ribbons, while your elastics hang over the buttons.

A pretty and **USEFUL DECORATION** for your room!

In this project, you will use:

Running stitch (see page 115)

French knots (see page 118)

Sewing on buttons (see page 116)

Using a pattern (see page 114)

You will need:

Paper and a pencil

Scissors

Brown felt

Pins

Embroidery floss (thread) and a needle

Fiberfill (stuffing)

3 lengths of ribbon, each about 8 inches (20 cm) long and about ½ inch (1 cm) wide

Colored felt

Needle and thread

Narrow ribbon for the loop

3 large colorful buttons

1 Photocopy the templates on page 127 at double the size, then cut out a paper pattern for a flowerpot, a flower, and a leaf. Fold the brown felt in half and pin the flowerpot pattern onto it. Cut around the pattern. Remove the pins and pattern. You now have two flowerpot shapes. Pin them together.

2 Cut a length of embroidery floss and tie a knot at one end. Thread the needle. Starting at the back of one of the bottom corners of the flowerpot, sew running stitch around the sides and top of the pot. Finish with a knot on the back. Remove the pins and trim the floss.

3 Stuff the pot with Fiberfill, pushing it into the corners with the wrong end of a pencil.

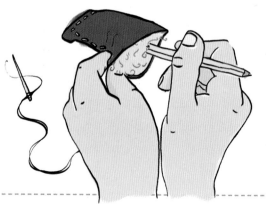

4 Pin the ribbons inside the bottom of the pot. Cut another length of embroidery floss and thread the needle. Starting and finishing with a knot on the back of the pot, sew running stitch across the bottom of the pot. Be sure to stitch through the ribbons. Trim the floss. Remove the pins as you work.

5 Pin the flower and leaf patterns onto colored felt and cut around them. Remove the pins and patterns. Keep cutting out flowers and leaves until you have about seven flowers and six leaves.

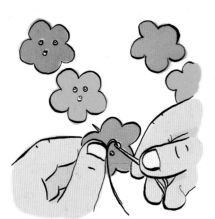

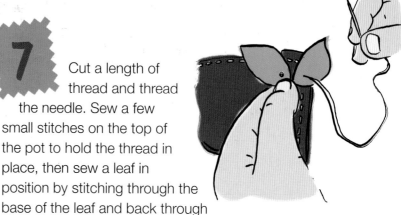

7 Cut a length of thread and thread the needle. Sew a few small stitches on the top of the pot to hold the thread in place, then sew a leaf in position by stitching through the base of the leaf and back through the pot. Finish with a few small stitches. Trim the thread.

Sew a flower onto the pot in the same way, stitching through the center of the flower. Try to keep the stitches small so that they will hardly show on the front of the flower. Sew the rest of the leaves and flowers onto the pot in the same way, overlapping them to make them look pretty.

6 Thread the needle with floss and, starting and finishing with a knot on the back of the felt, sew French knots in the center of each of the flowers. Trim the floss.

8 Now make a loop to hang up your barrette holder. Thread the needle with another piece of thread. Make a loop from the piece of narrow ribbon. Starting with a few small stitches in the felt, stitch the ribbon onto the back of the top of the pot, stitching through both layers of ribbon. Finish with a few small stitches, then trim the thread.

9 Sew a button onto the end of each ribbon.

Hang up all your hair accessories on the holder!

Hanging felt stars

Homemade Christmas tree decorations are always the best. Make these colorful green and red stars to hang on your tree this Christmas. These stars are decorated with pretty buttons, but you could use sequins instead to make them shine.

Stars to BRIGHTEN YOUR CHRISTMAS tree!

In this project, you will use:

Using a pattern (see page 114)

Running stitch (see page 115)

You will need:

Paper and a pencil

Scissors

Colored felt

Pins

Pinking shears

6 inches (15 cm) rickrack per decoration

A needle

Cotton thread to match the felt

Fiberfill (stuffing)

Craft glue

Assorted pearl buttons or sequins to decorate

1 Photocopy the template on page 124 at double the size, then cut out the paper pattern. Fold the felt in half, as you will need two star shapes per decoration. Pin the pattern to the felt and use a pencil to draw around it.

2 Remove the pattern, but pin the two pieces of felt together again before you start cutting. Using pinking shears, carefully cut all the way around the star shape. The pinking shears give a zigzag effect to the edges. Cut out as many stars as you want to make.

3 To make the hanging loop, fold a 6-inch (15-cm) length of rickrack in half and place it between the two layers of felt at the top of one of the points. Thread the needle. Start with a few small stitches in the top layer of felt to secure the thread and then push the needle through the two layers of felt, and the two layers of rickrack. Sew two or three stitches through all four layers to secure the loop.

4 Continue stitching around the points of the star using small running stitches about ¼ inch (5 mm) from the edge. Leave one side of the last point open for the stuffing.

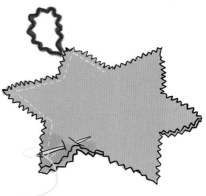

5 Carefully push the Fiberfill into the opening. You may need to use the sharp end of a pencil to push the stuffing right into the points of the star.

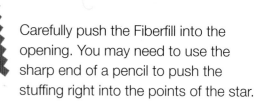

6 Stitch the opening closed using small running stitches ¼ inch (5 mm) from the edges of the felt. Finish off with a few small finishing stitches and trim the thread.

7 Use neat dabs of glue to stick the buttons or sequins to the front of the star, then leave to dry completely. If you have enough buttons or sequins, stick some on the other side, too—but only when the first side is completely dry.

Rickrack fairy

This funny, friendly fairy will be able to sit at the top of your Christmas tree. You'll be able to use her year after year. Perhaps you could make up a story all about how she got the job!

In this project, you will use:

Backstitch (see page 115)

French knots (see page 118)

Sewing on buttons (see page 116)

You will need:

Squared paper, plain paper, and a pencil

Cream fabric for the head

Colored fabrics for the body and skirt

Scissors

A needle and thread

Pins

Fiberfill (stuffing)

24 inches (60 cm) of ¼-inch (6-mm) wide gingham ribbon

14 inches (35 cm) rickrack

10 inches (25 cm) pom-pom fringe

Craft glue

Pink and blue embroidery floss and a needle

40 inches (1 m) gold rickrack for the hair

A scrap of white rickrack for the crown

3 pretty buttons

1 Using the squared paper, cut out two rectangles, one measuring 2½ x 10¼ inches (6 x 26 cm) and one measuring 3½ x 10¼ inches (9 x 26 cm). Pin the smaller rectangle to the cream fabric and cut around it. Lay the two different-colored fabrics on top of each other, pin the bigger rectangle to them, and cut around it.

2 Choose which fabric will be for the body and which will be for the skirt. With right sides facing, sew one long side of the cream fabric and one long side of the body fabric together, using backstitch. Then sew one long side of the skirt fabric to the other long side of the body fabric in the same way. Ask an adult to help you press the seam open.

3 Photocopy the template on page 127 at double the size, then cut out a pattern for the fairy. Fold the fabric panel in half and lay the paper pattern across it as shown. Pin the pattern to the fabric and cut around it.

4

With right sides facing, pin the two pieces together. Thread the needle and, beginning with a few small stitches in one bottom corner, use backstitch to sew around the fairy to the other corner. Leave the bottom open. Turn right side out and fill with Fiberfill.

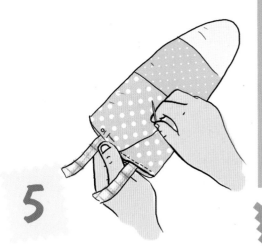

5

Cut two pieces of gingham ribbon for the legs, each 2 inches (5 cm) long. Turn the raw fabric edges along the bottom of the fairy to the inside and put the top of the ribbons inside the opening. Pin into position. Close the opening with backstitch, starting and finishing with a few small stitches to hold the thread in place. Trim the thread and remove the pins.

6

Measure how much rickrack you will need to go around the fairy's neck. Cut it a little longer so there is enough to overlap the ends.

Spread some newspaper over the table and stretch out the rickrack on top of it. Put something heavy on each end to hold it down flat and tight. Carefully trickle a very thin line of glue all along it. Press the rickrack on around the neck seam, overlapping the ends at the back. Do the same for the waist of the fairy and then glue a length of pom-pom fringe around the bottom of the skirt, each time overlapping the ends at the back.

7 Thread the needle with blue embroidery floss and knot the end. Starting at the back of the fairy's head, push the needle through to the front and embroider a French knot for one eye. Take the needle underneath her face to the position of the other eye and embroider another French knot. Push the needle back through to the back of her head and finish with a knot. Then, re-thread the needle with pink floss and, starting at the back of the head again, sew a few small pink stitches to form the mouth. Finish with a knot at the back of the head.

8 Cut eight 5-inch (12.5-cm) lengths of gold rickrack for the fairy's hair. Thread the needle with embroidery floss and sew a few stitches on the top of the fairy's head. Arrange the rickrack pieces across her head and stitch over them a few times to hold them in place.

9 Measure a piece of white rickrack to go around the fairy's head for a crown. Sew a button to the center. Glue the rickrack around the head, overlapping the ends at the back. Stitch a button onto each leg ribbon.

10 Finally, find the center of the remaining gingham ribbon by folding it in half. Stitch the center of the ribbon to the back of the fairy with a few small stitches. Then tie your fairy to the top of the Christmas tree with a large bow, which will look like wings!

Christmas stocking

Hang up this pretty stocking and you are sure to tempt Santa to fill it with something special. On the other hand, it would make a lovely gift for someone else at Christmas.

In this project, you will use:

Using a pattern (see page 114)

Running stitch (see page 115)

Blanket stitch (see page 116)

You will need:

Paper and a pencil

Scissors

18 inches (45 cm) cream wool fabric, 54 inches (137 cm) wide

Pins

Felt for heart (6 x 6 inches/ 15 x 15 cm)

A needle

White thread

Red thread

Red embroidery floss (thread)

10 inches (26 cm) gingham fabric, 54 inches (137 cm) wide

4 inches (10 cm) gingham ribbon

Pearl button

Craft glue

1 Photocopy the stocking template on page 125 at double the size and cut it out to make the pattern. Fold the cream wool fabric in half and pin the stocking pattern to the fabric. Cut out the two stocking pieces.

2 Photocopy the heart template on page 120 at double the size and cut it out to make a pattern. Pin the heart pattern to the felt and cut out a heart shape to decorate the front of the stocking.

3 Thread the needle with white cotton and baste (tack) the heart to the front stocking piece. (Baste means use big running stitches, which you will pull out later, to hold the heart in place.)

4 Now thread the needle with red thread and work small blanket stitches all the way around the heart. When you have finished, carefully pull out the basting.

5 With right sides facing, stitch the two stocking pieces together using running stitch. Then, on the curves of the toe and heel, use a pair of sharp scissors to make little snips toward the line of stitching, being careful not to cut into your stitches. This will help the fabric turn around the curves.

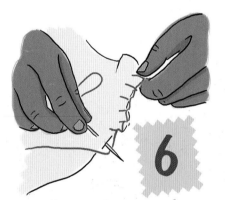

6 Turn the stocking right side out. Thread a needle with the red embroidery floss and sew blanket stitch all the way around the edges of the stocking, leaving the top edges open. Ask an adult to help you press the stocking flat with an iron.

7 You will also need help from an adult with the next stages because there is a lot of pressing to do. First, draw a rectangle 24½ x 8 inches (62 x 20 cm) on the gingham fabric, using the squares to help keep the sides straight. Cut it out.

Now place the gingham right side down on an ironing board and turn over a hem of ½ inch (1 cm) along both the long edges. Press the hems flat. Thread your needle and sew running stitch along these two hems. Now turn in a ½-inch (1-cm) hem at both ends and press them flat. Stitch running stitch along these hems, too.

8 Next, fold the gingham in half lengthwise, wrong sides together (all the hems inside), and press it flat.

9 Fit the folded gingham over the top of the stocking with it half in and half outside the stocking. The two ends should touch or overlap slightly at the back seam. Sew a line of running stitch around the top of the stocking to hold the gingham in place.

10 Fold the piece of gingham ribbon in half to form a loop. Stitch it to the inside of the stocking at the back seam, stitching through the gingham and the stocking.

11 Finally, use a dab of glue to stick the pearl button to the very center of the heart.

Lavender bags

This is one of the easiest of the sewing projects and one of the loveliest, especially if it's summer and you have a lavender bush in your garden. But remember——you will have to wait for the lavender to dry before you can use it. Make the bags in pretty floral fabrics and soft pastel colors to give them an old-fashioned look.

In this project, you will use:

Running stitch (see page 115)

You will need:

Dried lavender heads (you can buy them or collect and dry your own)

A tray and paper, if drying your own lavender

Squared paper

Pinking shears

Floral fabric

Embroidery floss (thread)

A needle

A teaspoon

10 inches (25 cm) narrow ribbon per bag

Scissors

1 If you have a lavender bush flowering in your garden, carefully use scissors to snip off the long stems of lavender flowers. Cover a tray with a sheet of paper and place the lavender on top. Spread the stems out well and put the tray in a warm, dark, dry place until the flowers have dried completely (an airing cupboard is good for this). Drying will take several weeks.

When the flowers are dry, carefully pull them off the stalks and collect them in a bowl.

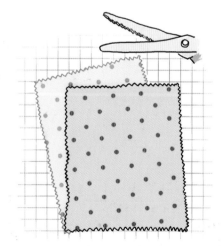

2 On the squared paper, draw a 5 x 8-inch (12 x 40-cm) rectangle and cut it out. Fold the fabric in half and pin the pattern to the fabric. Using pinking shears, cut around the pattern to give you two rectangles. (The pinking shears give a pretty edge and will also prevent the fabric from fraying.)

3 Pin the two rectangles together with wrong sides facing. Cut a length of embroidery floss that is a different color to your fabric and thread the needle. Starting with a few small stitches to secure the thread, stitch all the way around three sides of the bag using running stitch. Leave the top open. The stitches should be no more than ½ inch (1 cm) apart, so that the lavender will not leak out. Finish with a few small stitches.

4 Using a teaspoon, carefully fill the bag with lavender flowers. Fill the bag to about halfway up. Make sure it is quite plump and full.

5 Lay the lavender bag down on its side and wrap the ribbon around the bag, just above the lavender. Tie a bow and then trim the ends using scissors.

CHAPTER FOUR

Gifts and cards

Felt egg cozies

Give your Easter egg ears! These colorful egg cozies with their funny bunny ears will keep your eggs warm and make you smile at Easter.

1 Trace the egg cozy template on page 122 onto paper and cut out the pattern. Pin the pattern to the felt and cut out two pieces of felt for each egg cozy.

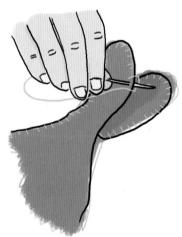

2 Pin the two pieces of felt together in the lower part, where the egg will go. Choose an embroidery floss that is a contrasting color to the felt, thread your needle, and tie a knot. Starting on the inside of the egg cozy, pull the needle through to the outside and blanket stitch up one side from the bottom edge to the base of the ears.

3 When you reach the ears, keep them separate as two ears. Continue to blanket stitch around one ear, sewing through just one layer of felt to decorate it. Do the same around the other ear and then continue in blanket stitch down the other side of the egg cozy through both layers of felt.

For this project, you will use:

Blanket stitch (see page 116)

Using a pattern (see page 114)

You will need:

Scissors

Pins

10 x 10 inches (25 x 25 cm) felt per egg cozy

Embroidery floss (thread)

A sewing needle

Felt flowers to decorate

3-D fabric paint (optional)

Fabric glue

An egg cozy to MAKE YOU SMILE!

4

If you are using the 3-D fabric paint, make a small dot in the center of each scallop along the bottom of the egg cozy. Do one side and let it dry—this can take about an hour. When it is dry, repeat on the other side of the egg cozy.

5

Use fabric glue to stick felt flowers to each side of the egg cozy. Allow the glue to dry completely.

Ribbon bouquet card

Is it coming up to Mother's Day or is your sister getting married? Make a truly special card for a special occasion, using ribbon embroidery.

A beautiful card for a **SPECIAL OCCASION!**

In this project, you will use:

Backstitch (see page 116)

You will need:

Paper and a pencil

Sticky tape

A thin piece of cream card

Narrow ⅛-inch (3-mm) ribbon in pretty flower colors

An embroidery needle

Scissors

Pale green embroidery floss (thread)

8½ x 11-inch (A4) piece of thicker colored card

A glue stick

1 Cut out a rectangle of cream card measuring 6¾ x 4¼ inches (17 x 11 cm). Photocopy or trace the design for the embroidery on page 123.

You'll need a sunny day for the next stage. Use a couple of pieces of sticky tape to tape the design pattern onto a window. Hold the cream card over the top. You should be able to see the design through the card. Lightly trace over the design in pencil.

2

Cut a length of ribbon and thread it through the needle. Tie a double knot in the end. Starting from the back, bring the needle through the card in the position of the first flower. Stitch the flower petals over the pencil lines.

The flowers have different color centers and petals so, before you finish off, take the needle underneath the

card to the center of one of the other flowers and stitch two stitches. Finish on the back with a knot.

Now thread your needle with another color ribbon and stitch a second flower and a different center. Stitch the last flower and the last center in the third color. Trim the ends of the ribbon on the back of the card.

4

Thread the needle with green embroidery floss and tie a knot at the end. Starting from the back of the card, embroider lines of small back stitches along the flower stems.

5 Thread the needle with a 7-inch (18-cm) length of pink ribbon. Push it through from the front of the card to the back and through to the front again, without a knot, and tie into a small bow. Trim the ends of the ribbon to the same length.

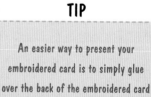

6 Score the piece of colored card across the center and fold it in half. If you want a cut-out frame for your card, place the embroidered card carefully in the center of the inside front of the folded card and draw around it. Draw another rectangle with sides about ¼ inch (1 cm) in from the sides of the first one. Ask an adult to cut this rectangle out using a craft knife. Glue around the inside of the frame and push the embroidered card against it. You may need to add a little sticky tape on the inside to hold it firm.

> **TIP**
>
> An easier way to present your embroidered card is to simply glue over the back of the embroidered card and press it firmly to the front of the folded colored card, leaving a border all around it. Put a book on top of it to weigh it down until it is dry.

Finger puppet card

A greetings card and a present all in one, these finger-puppet greetings cards are great for younger brothers, sisters, or cousins. You can make the characters shown here or use the basic pattern and invent your own heroes and villains.

In this project, you will use:

Using a pattern (see page 114)

Running stitch (see page 115)

Cross stitch (see page 118)

You will need:

Paper and a pencil

Scissors

Flesh-colored felt

Scraps of felt in different colors

Craft glue

Pins

Embroidery flosses (threads) and a needle

Yarn (wool) for hair

Thin card in pastel colors

Adhesive pads

1 Photocopy the templates on page 127 at double the size and then cut out the pieces you need for your finger puppet character. Fold the flesh-colored felt in half and pin the basic puppet shape to it. Cut it out to give you two puppet shapes. Pin the clothes patterns to a single layer of felt and cut them out.

2 Glue the clothes to the front of the puppet, using craft glue. Cut some short lengths of yarn and glue in place as the hair. Leave to dry. Leave the hat off until later.

3 Cut a length of black, brown, or blue embroidery floss and tie a knot in the end. Starting from the wrong side, embroider a cross stitch for each eye. Finish on the wrong side with a knot.

Now thread the needle with red floss, tie a knot, and embroider another cross stitch for the mouth. Finish off on the wrong side with another knot.

4 Pin the front of the puppet to the back. Thread the needle with embroidery floss to match your puppet's clothes and tie a knot. Starting with the knot on the inside of the puppet, stitch the two sides together using small running stitches. Finish off with another knot inside the puppet. Now glue on the hat!

5 Cut a piece of card measuring 6 x 8¼ inches (15 x 21 cm) and fold it in half. Using felt and the templates from page 127, cut out the background shapes for each puppet.

6 Stick the shapes onto the card using craft glue and leave to dry. Attach the finger puppet to the card with an adhesive pad.

Glasses case

Is your grandmother forever looking for her glasses? A great gift, this fun glasses case is quick and easy to make and so brightly colored it will never get lost.

A glasses case that will NEVER GET LOST!

In this project, you will use:

Using a pattern (see page 114)

Running stitch (see page 115)

You will need:

Paper and a pencil

Scissors

12 x 12 inches (30 x 30 cm) colored felt

Pins

Pinking shears

A needle

Embroidery floss (thread)

A ruler

8 inches (20 cm) rickrack or braid

Glue

1 Photocopy the glasses case template on page 125 at double the size, then cut out the pattern. Fold the felt in half. Pin the pattern to the felt and cut around it, using pinking shears to give a zigzag edge. Remove the pattern.

2 Pin the two sides of the glasses case together with wrong sides facing. Thread a needle with embroidery floss and tie a knot. Starting just inside the glasses case, pull your needle through to the front and then, using quite big running stitches, sew all the way around the outside edge of the case. Your stitches should be about ½ inch (1 cm) long. Finish with a knot on the inside. Remember to leave the top straight edge of the glasses case open.

3 Now stick on the rickrack. Using a ruler, draw a line about ¾ inch (2 cm) from the open edge of the glasses case on both sides. Spread some newspaper over the table and lay the rickrack on top of it. Put something heavy on each end to hold it down flat and tight. Trickle a very thin line of glue along it for 4 inches (10 cm) in the middle of the rickrack.

4 Press the glued rickrack onto the line on the front of the glasses case. Turn the case over. Trickle glue along the two ends of the rickrack and press them down along the line at the back of the glasses case so that they overlap in the middle. Leave the glue to dry completely.

Garden tote

This practical yet pretty garden tote is the perfect gift for a new gardener or even a keen one, especially if you fill it with packets of seeds and seed markers. It is made of natural burlap (hessian) fabric and painted with garden designs of vegetables or flowers.

In this project, you will use:

Using a pattern (see page 114)

Running stitch (see page 115)

Slipstitch (see page 117)

You will need:

Large paper and squared paper

A ruler and pencil

20 inches (54 cm) burlap (hessian) fabric, approximately 54 inches (137 cm) wide

Scissors

Fabric paint in flower or vegetable colors

A fine paintbrush

Pins

Lime green and brown embroidery floss (thread)

A needle

An iron and ironing board (ask an adult)

Iron-on fusible interlining

1 On the squared paper, draw and cut out four 4-inch (10-cm) squares for the pockets and two 10 x 3-inch (25 x 8-cm) rectangles for the handles. Photocopy the template on page 124 at double the size for the oval for the base and cut it out. Cut a large paper rectangle, 22 x 7 inches (55 x 18 cm), for the main bag.

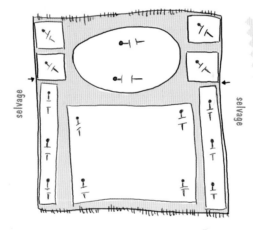

2 Lay the burlap out flat and pin the pattern pieces on, as shown, so that the tops of two of the pockets and one long edge of each handle piece are laid along each selvage (the non-fraying side of the fabric).

3 On the three non-selvage sides of each pocket, carefully pull away strands of burlap to fray the edges to about ½ inch (1 cm) from each side.

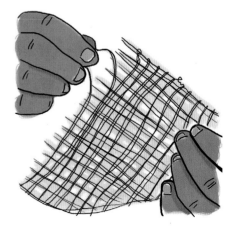

4 Use a brush to paint a design on each of the pockets with fabric paints. Fix the paint following the manufacturer's instructions. (This usually involves ironing, so ask an adult to help you.) Put to one side.

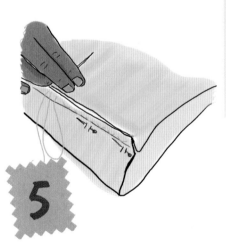

5

Fold the main bag piece in half and pin it together. Thread your needle with brown embroidery floss. Starting with a few small stitches to secure the thread, stitch the side seam using small running stitches ½ inch (1 cm) from the edge. Finish with a few small stitches.

6 Ask an adult to help you press both layers of the seam to one side with an iron. Then, using brown embroidery floss and starting and finishing with a few small stitches, stitch a row of running stitches along this seam to prevent the edges from fraying. Be careful not to stitch into the other side of the bag.

7 Ask an adult to iron the fusible interlining to one side of the burlap oval and then trim the edges to the oval shape. Now, with right sides together (so that the seam and the interfacing are on the outside), pin the oval to the bag. Thread the needle with more brown embroidery thread and, starting and finishing with a few small stitches, stitch around the base of the bag using running stitch. Afterwards, slipstitch around the raw edges to prevent them from fraying.

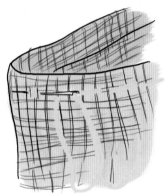

8 Turn the bag right side out and then fold the top of the bag 1½ inches (3 cm) to the inside. Ask an adult to help you press it flat with an iron. Thread your needle with green embroidery floss and, starting and finishing with a few small stitches, use running stitch to sew this hem in place.

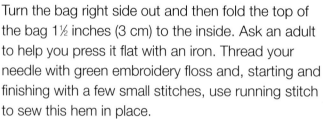

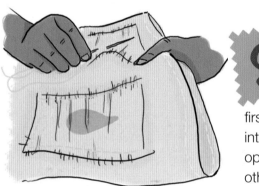

9 Now pin the pockets in position on both sides. Thread your needle with green embroidery floss and, starting with a few stitches over and over at the top corner of the first pocket, stitch it into position using small running stitches. Stitch into the un-frayed part of the pocket and leave the selvage edge open. Finish with a few more small stitches over and over at the other top corner.

10 You will need some more adult help when you make the handles. Lay one handle section flat on the ironing board and turn the ends in by ½ inch (1 cm) and press. Fold and press the long, non-selvage edge in by 1 inch (2.5 cm). Then fold and press the selvage edge in by 1 inch (2.5 cm) flat over the top of that. Do the same for the other handle. Stitch along the length of the handles with running stitches, using the green floss.

11 Pin the handles to the inside of the bag above the pockets, with the ends about 5 inches (12 cm) apart. Thread the needle with brown floss and stitch the ends of the handles to the inside of the bag using slipstitch to hold them securely in place.

Sausage dog draft excluder

This adorable sausage dog can lie along the bottom of your door to keep out cold drafts or it can lie on your bed as a huggable friend. Whatever it's for, it's easy to make from an old pair of pantyhose. The one in the photo has a pair of old mittens for ears, but socks would work just as well.

In this project, you will use:

Running stitch (see page 115)

Slipstitch (see page 117)

Sewing on buttons (see page 116)

Using a pattern (see page 114)

You will need:

An old pair of woolen pantyhose (tights)

Scissors

Fiberfill (stuffing)

Yarn (wool)

A needle with a large eye

Paper and a pencil

Old mittens or clean old socks (ask first)

Scraps of fabric

Pins

2 buttons

1 Cut one of the legs from an old pair of woolen pantyhose. Cut as high up as you can to make the dog as long as possible.

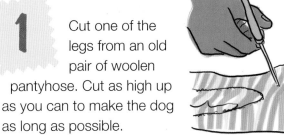

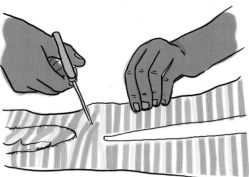

2 Stuff the cut leg of the pantyhose with Fiberfill. Push it right into the toe first. Push each handful of Fiberfill as far down as you can before adding the next, so that it forms a smooth sausage shape. Don't fill it all the way to the top.

3

Cut a length of yarn and tie it firmly around the end of the sausage, finishing with a double knot to hold it in place.

4

At the other end, tie another piece of yarn around the toe to make a big doggy nose. Again, tie a double knot to hold the nose in place.

5

Thread your needle with a length of yarn and knot the end. Using running stitch, sew a mitten onto each side of the sausage, by the heel of the panty hose, to make the dog's ears. If you have no mittens, cut the foot parts off an old pair of socks and use these instead.

6

Trace the heart-shaped template on page 121 onto paper and cut it out. Pin the pattern onto a scrap of fabric and cut round it. Repeat until you have as many hearts as you want to sew onto your dog. Pin them to the dog.

A long, cuddly, **ADORABLE** *sausage dog!*

7 Thread the needle with more yarn and tie a knot in the end. Sew the hearts onto the dog using slipstitch. Finish with a knot.

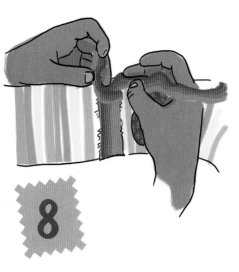

8 Sew the buttons onto the dog for eyes. Tear a strip off some fabric or use a piece of ribbon and tie it around the sausage dog's neck to make his collar.

Needle case

Keep needles safe in this pretty cherry needle case. It's easy to make and a "must have" for your sewing kit—but if you can bear to give it away, it would make a perfect gift.

You'll **NEVER LOSE YOUR NEEDLES** again!

In this project, you will use:

Sewing on buttons (see page 116)

Running stitch (see page 115)

You will need:

Squared paper (for example, from a math book)

Pencil

Ruler

Scissors

Pins

Felt in 3 colors

Pinking shears (optional)

Narrow green ribbon, about 12 inches (30 cm) long

Green and red embroidery floss (thread) and a needle

2 red buttons

1 Draw a rectangle measuring 6¾ x 4¼ inches (17 x 11 cm) on the squared paper. Cut it out and pin it to one of the felt pieces. Cut around the paper using pinking shears to give a zigzag edge. (Use ordinary scissors if you don't have pinking shears—the case will still look pretty.) This will be the cover of the needle case. Remove the pins and pattern.

2 Draw another rectangle measuring 3½ x 2¾ inches (9 x 7 cm) on the squared paper. Cut it out and pin it to another color of felt. Cut around the paper using the pinking shears (if you have them). This will be the background for the cherry decoration on the front of the case. Remove the pins and the pattern.

3 Take the ribbon and tie a bow in it. Trim the ends so that they are about 1½ inches (4 cm) long. Cut a length of green floss and knot it at one end. Thread the needle. Starting with the knot on the underside, use a few small stitches to stitch the ribbon onto the smaller felt rectangle. Finish with another knot on the back of the felt. Trim the thread.

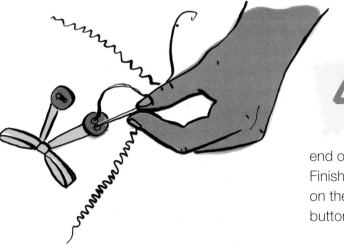

4 Thread the needle with red floss and, beginning with a few small stitches on the back of the ribbon, sew a red button onto one end of the ribbon so that it looks like a cherry. Finish with a few more small stitches on the back of the ribbon. Sew the other button onto the other end of the ribbon.

5 Take the larger felt rectangle (the cover) from Step 1 and fold it in half like a book. Position the cherry felt on the front cover and pin it in place, taking care to pin only through the front cover of the book and not the back. Open the book out again so it is flat.

Now cut a length of green embroidery floss and tie a knot at one end. Thread the needle. Starting with the knot at the back of the cover, sew on the cherry felt using running stitch. Finish with a knot on the back. Trim the floss.

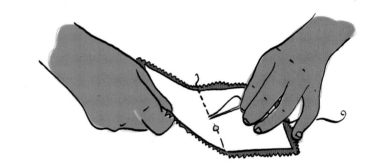

6 Draw another rectangle measuring 6 x 3¾ inches (15 x 9.5 cm) on the squared paper. Cut it out and pin it to the third piece of felt. Cut out the felt with scissors. This will make the pages in the needle case. Remove the pins and pattern.

Fold the felt for the pages in half to find the middle. Now fold the cover in half again and pin the middle of the pages to the middle of the cover. Cut a length of red embroidery floss and tie a knot at one end. Thread the needle. Starting from the back of the pages, sew running stitch up the middle to hold them in place. Finish with a knot on the back of the pages. Trim the floss. Remove the pins.

Patchwork pincushion

Every stitcher needs a pincushion and this is the prettiest one you're ever likely to find. It is a perfect introduction to patchwork and only needs the smallest scraps of fabric to make.

1 Photocopy the templates on page 126 at double the size and cut them out. Pin the segment pattern onto your first fabric scrap and cut around it. Cut out six segment pieces for the top of the pincushion and six for the bottom from scraps of several different fabrics. Lay them on your work surface to make two circles and move them around until you are happy with the design.

In this project, you will use:

Using a pattern (see page 114)

Backstitch (see page 115)

Slipstitch (see page 117)

Running stitch (see page 115)

Sewing on buttons (see page 116)

You will need:

Paper and a pencil

Scraps of fabric

A needle and thread

Fiberfill (stuffing)

Embroidery floss (thread) and a needle

A pretty button

2 Start with the top of the pincushion. With right sides together, pin two segments together. Thread the needle and, beginning with a few small stitches to hold the thread in place, stitch the two segments together using small backstitches. Finish with a few small finishing stitches and trim the thread. Remove the pins.

With right sides together sew on another segment in the same way to make a semi-circle. Try to keep your stitching exactly the same distance from the edge of the fabric on each seam that you sew. Put the first semi-circle to one side and stitch the other three segments together to form a second semi-circle. Ask an adult to help you press all the seams open.

3

With right sides together, pin and stitch the two semi-circles together along their straight edge to form a circle. Ask an adult to help you press the seam open. Repeat steps 2 and 3 with the other six segments to make the bottom circle of the pincushion.

Your very first PATCHWORK!

4

With right sides together, pin the two fabric circles together, making sure that the joins on the top and bottom circles line up. Stitch the two circles together using small backstitches. Leave an opening of about 1 inch (2.5 cm) for stuffing.

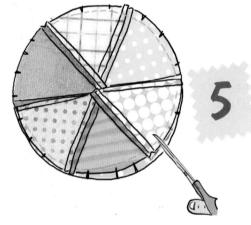

5

Make small snips all the way around in the seam to help the seam make a curve. Be very careful not to snip through your stitching. Turn the pincushion the right way out. Ask an adult to help you press it again.

6

Stuff the cushion with small pieces of Fiberfill. Use the blunt end of a pencil to help you push the stuffing in. When it is nice and full, turn the raw edges of the opening to the inside and close up the opening using small slipstitches.

TIP

You will need a long piece of embroidery floss for the loops in step 7. If you begin to run out of floss, stitch a few small finishing stitches at the top center and trim the thread. Cut another length of floss and knot it. Begin at the top center again, go down to the bottom and up again, and then continue with the loops. Finish with a few stitches at the top center.

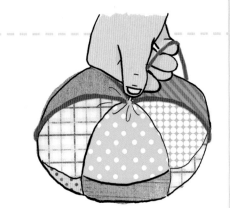

7

Cut a long length of embroidery floss and tie a knot in the end. Thread the needle, push it through the center of the top of the cushion, and pull it out through the center of the bottom. Bring the needle back up to the top and, this time, take it around the outside of the cushion in a big loop and back up through the bottom to the top.

Pull the loop so that it lines up with a fabric join. Pull it quite tight so that the middle of the pincushion is squeezed in. From the top, loop the floss around the outside along the next fabric join into the bottom and back out of the top again.

Keep going until you have a line of floss along each of the fabric joins. Finish with a few small stitches at the top center.

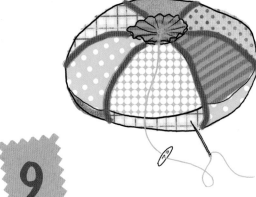

8

Now for the center decoration. Pin the pattern to a piece of fabric and cut around it. Remove the pins and pattern. Thread the needle and, starting with a few small stitches, sew running stitch all the way round the edge about ⅛ inch (3 mm) in from the edge. Gently pull the thread, gathering the fabric to form a small yo-yo. Finish with a few small stitches to hold it in place.

9

Thread the needle again and sew a few small stitches in the center of the pincushion. Sew the yo-yo in place, stitching up through the yo-yo and back into the pincushion a few times. The next time, add in the button and stitch up through the button and down into the yo-yo a few times. Finally, push the needle right back through to the bottom of the pincushion and finish off with a few small stitches.

Sewing basket

Scissors, needles, pins, and thread can all be kept safe and tidy in this pretty and practical sewing basket. Two different color fabrics make it look special, but all one color looks lovely too.

In this project, you will use:

Running stitch (see page 115)

Gathering (see page 117)

You will need:

Round metal cookie tin, about 7 inches (18 cm) in diameter

Cardboard

A ballpoint pen

Scissors

One square of fabric with sides about 28 inches (72 cm) long

One square of fabric with sides about 12 inches (30 cm) long

A tape measure

A needle and thread

Craft glue

Rickrack

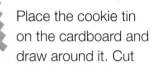

1 Place the cookie tin on the cardboard and draw around it. Cut out the cardboard just inside the pen line, so that the cardboard circle is slightly smaller than the tin. Check that it fits loosely inside the cookie tin—if it's tight, trim it a little more. Put the cardboard to one side.

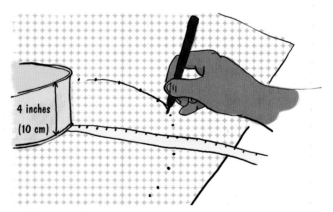

4 inches (10 cm)

2 Place the larger piece of fabric wrong side up on a table. Place the cookie tin right in the middle and draw around it.

Now for some math! Using the tape measure, measure the depth of the tin. Double this measurement. Now add on 1½ inches (4 cm). Write down the total and check it. Next, using the tape measure, measure this total out from the edge of the circle and make a mark on the fabric with the pen. Do the same a bit further round. Keep going marking this distance from the circle all the way round it. Join the dots to draw a much bigger circle around the first circle. Cut around the big outer circle.

HERE'S THE MATH FOR STEP 2!

4 inches + 4 inches + 1½ inches = 9½ inches

10 cm + 10 cm + 4 cm = 24 cm

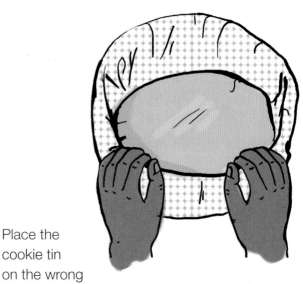

3 Cut a length of thread and thread the needle. Sew a few small starting stitches near the edge of the fabric and then sew large running stitches all the way around the circle.

4 Place the cookie tin on the wrong side of the fabric in the middle of the circle. Gently pull the thread and gather up the fabric around it. Push the fabric neatly into the base of the tin, so that the tin is completely covered except for a small circle on the bottom inside. Finish with a few small stitches. Trim the thread. Arrange the folds evenly around the tin.

5 Next make the base of your basket. Lay the second piece of fabric on the table, wrong side up. Place the cardboard circle right in the middle and draw around it with the pen. This time measure out 1½ inches (4 cm) from the circle all the way around it and join the dots to make another, slightly bigger circle. Cut around this bigger circle.

6 Cut a length of thread and thread the needle. Sew a few small starting stitches near the edge of the fabric and then sew large running stitches all the way around the circle, just as in Step 3.

7 Now put the cardboard circle on the wrong side of the fabric in the middle of the circle. Gently pull the thread and gather the fabric over the cardboard circle. Finish with a few small stitches in the fabric. Trim the thread. Arrange the folds evenly around the cardboard.

Keep your needles and thread SAFE AND TIDY!

8

Dab craft glue inside the base of the cookie tin and on the underside of the covered cardboard circle. Push this circle down onto the bottom of the tin to give a neat finish to your basket. Put something heavy inside the container until the glue dries (a bag of dried beans or rice will work well).

9

Use the tape measure to measure about 1 inch (2.5 cm) from the top of the tin and make a small dot with the pen. Do this in several places around the tin. The dots will be a guide to help you glue the rickrack on straight.

Now measure how much rickrack you will need to go around the tin and cut it a little longer so there is enough to overlap the ends. Spread some newspaper over the table and stretch the rickrack on top of it. Put something heavy on each end to hold it down flat and tight. Carefully trickle a very thin line of glue all along it.

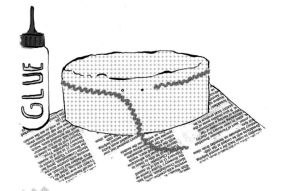

10

Press the rickrack onto the tin covering the pen marks. Overlap the ends. If the rickrack seems to be slipping, pin through it in a few places and remove the pins when the glue is dry.

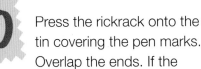

Fill your basket with all your sewing things!

Sewing techniques

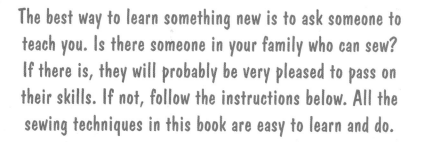

The best way to learn something new is to ask someone to teach you. Is there someone in your family who can sew? If there is, they will probably be very pleased to pass on their skills. If not, follow the instructions below. All the sewing techniques in this book are easy to learn and do.

Basic techniques

Using a pattern
There are lots of templates in this book to help you make patterns for the projects. To use them:

1 Trace the template onto tracing paper or thin paper that you can see through and cut them out to make a pattern.

2 Pin this pattern onto your fabric, making sure that the fabric is flat with no creases. Position the pattern close to the edges of the fabric so that you don't waste any. Try to pin patterns, especially rectangles, in line with the tiny threads you can see in the fabric (on felt it doesn't matter). If you need two pieces that are the same shape, fold the fabric over and pin the pattern so the pins go through both layers.

3 If the pattern has a dotted fold line on it, fold the fabric over and pin the pattern piece onto it, positioning the fold line on the pattern along the fold of the fabric. Cut around the pattern as close to the edge as you can.

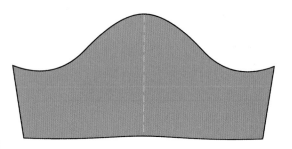

4 Remove the pins and the pattern. When the shape is opened out, it will be doubled.

How to use half-size templates
Some of the templates (on pages 124–127) need to be doubled in size to make the pattern big enough.
Ask somebody to photocopy the template for you, using the 200% zoom button on the photocopier.

Threading a needle
You won't be able to start sewing without threading your needle!

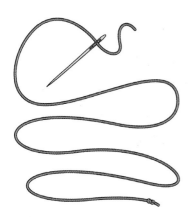

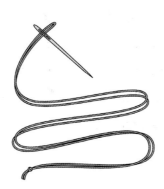

1 Thread your needle with about 25 inches (65 cm) of thread or yarn (wool). Pull about 6 inches (15 cm) of the thread through the needle. Tie two knots on top of each other at the other end.

2 For a double thread, which is stronger, pull the thread through the needle until the thread is doubled over and tie a knot in the two ends together.

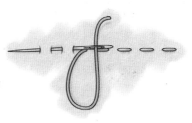

Running stitch
This is the simplest stitch and can be used in embroidery and for joining two layers of fabric together. It is very easy to do, but not very strong. Secure the end of the thread with a few small stitches. Push the needle down through the fabric a little way along, then bring it back up through the fabric a little further along. Repeat to form a row of stitches.

Backstitch
This is a very useful stitch, since it is strong and similar to the stitches used on a sewing machine. It makes a solid line of stitches.

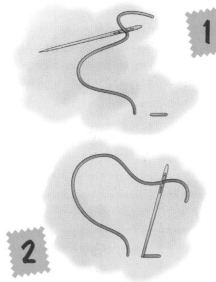

1 Start as if you were sewing running stitch. Sew one stitch and bring the needle back up to start the second stitch.

Finishing stitching
It is important to finish off all your stitching, so that it doesn't come undone.

When you have finished stitching, sew a few tiny stitches over and over in the same place on the back of the fabric. Then trim off your thread.

2 This time, instead of going forward, go back and push the needle through at the end of your first stitch.

3 Bring it out again a stitch length past the thread. Keep going to make an even line of stitches with no gaps.

Blanket stitch
This makes a pretty edge when you are sewing two layers of felt together.

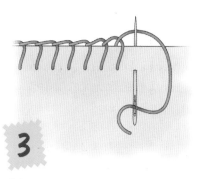

1

Bring the needle through at the edge of the fabric.

2

Push the needle back through the fabric a short distance from the edge and loop the thread under the needle. Pull the needle and thread as far as you can to make the first stitch.

3

Make another stitch to the right of this and again loop the thread under the needle. Continue along the fabric and finish with a few small stitches or a knot on the underside.

Sewing on buttons
You can use buttons as decorations—and you never know when you'll need to sew a button on some clothes!

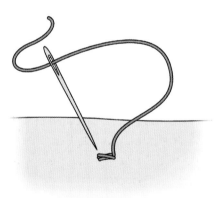

1 Mark the place where you want the button to go. Push the needle up from the back of the fabric and sew a few stitches over and over in this place.

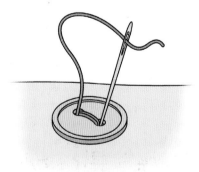

2 Now bring the needle up through one of the holes in the button. Push the needle back down through the second hole and through the fabric. Bring it back up through the first hole. Repeat this five or six times. If there are four holes in the button, use all four of them to make a cross pattern. Make sure that you keep the stitches close together under the middle of the button.

3 Finish with a few small stitches over and over on the back of the fabric and trim the thread.

Gathering

To create a fuller, ruffled effect with fabric, use this gathering technique.

1 To gather a piece of fabric, knot your thread and begin with a few small stitches over and over in the same place on the fabric to hold the thread firmly so it won't pull through.

2 Now sew a line of running stitches—the smaller the stitches, the smaller the gathers you will make.

3 At the end, don't finish off; leave the thread loose. Pull the fabric back along the line of stitches so it gathers up into folds.

4 When it is the right size, secure the end of the thread with a few stitches over and over in the same place so that the fabric can't come ungathered.

Slipstitch

This stitch is used to sew two layers of fabric together with stitches that show at the edges. It is also useful to close up a gap after stuffing an object. Begin with a knot or a few small stitches at the back of the two layers. Push the needle through both layers to the front, ⅛ inch (2–3 mm) from the edge, and pull the thread right through. Take the needle over the top to the back again and push it through to the front a little way along the seam. The stitches go over and over the edges of the two fabrics. Finish with a knot or a few small stitches.

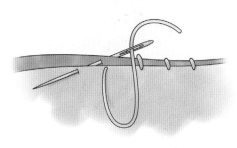

Decorative stitches

Cross stitch

You can use cross stitch for decorative details or to give a toy some eyes. To sew a single cross stitch, knot your thread, bring the needle up at A and down at B, then up at C and down at D. Knot again at the back.

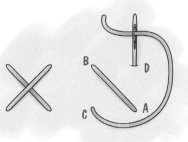

French knot

French knots are useful for sewing tiny eyes and the centers of flowers. They are a bit tricky, so practice on some scrap material first.

1 Knot your thread and bring the needle up from the back of the fabric to the front. Wrap the thread once or twice around the tip of the needle, then push the needle back in, right next to the place it came up.

2 As you push the needle in with one hand, hold the wrapped-around threads tightly against the fabric with the thumbnail of your other hand. Pull the needle all the way through. The wraps will form a knot on the surface of the fabric.

Chain stitch

This stitch makes a pretty line.

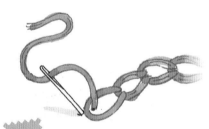

1 Knot the thread and bring the needle up from the back of the fabric. Push it back in right beside the place it came up and bring it out again a short distance away, looping the thread around the needle tip. Pull the thread through.

2 To begin the next stitch, push the needle down right beside the place at which it last came up, just inside the loop of the first chain, and bring it out a short distance away, again looping the thread around the needle tip. Keep going.

3 When you reach the end, bring your needle down outside the last loop to secure it and finish off on the back.

Single chain stitch

This is like chain stitch, but you only do one link of the chain. Stitch one link of the chain, then secure it with a tiny stitch across the top of the loop, just as in the last stitch of chain stitch.

Daisy stitch

This uses chain stitch to make a flower shape. Sew a group of six to eight single chain stitches in a circle to form a flower shape.

Fly stitch

This creates another pretty shape—you can do a single fly stitch or sew it in a row.

Bring the needle up at A and push it down at B, a short distance to the right, leaving a loose loop of thread. Bring the needle up at C, inside the loop, and push it down at D, outside the loop, to "tie" the loop in place.

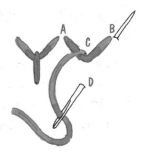

Chain and fly stitch

This stitch looks tricky, but with practice it's easy!

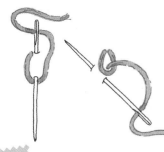

1 First, sew a single chain stitch.

2 Then sew a fly stitch which will make a V-shape at the base of the chain loop.

3 Tie the stitch down by sewing a small vertical stitch across the base of the V-shape.

Straight stitch

Straight stitches can be arranged to form other embroidery stitches, such as seed stitch and star stitch:

Seed stitch

Use these for a pretty, scattered effect. Sew pairs of very short straight stitches next to each other, scattering them all over in the space you want to fill.

Star stitch

Make star shapes using straight stitch. You can make your star even more special by sewing a French knot at the end of each point.

1 Draw a star shape on your fabric. Knot your thread and push the needle through the fabric at one of the outside points of the star.

2 Push your needle back through at the center of the star and then out again at the next outside point. Keep going until your star is complete and then finish off on the back.

Templates

For instructions on how to use these templates to make patterns, see page 114. All the templates on pages 120—121 are the correct size, so you can trace them (except the heart—read the note first!).

BUTTON BADGES

page 44

HEART

IMPORTANT NOTE: You can use this heart template for the Sausage dog draft excluder (page 101) and for the Christmas stocking (page 81). Trace it at this size for the sausage dog. For the Christmas stocking, **you will need to photocopy it at double the size** (see page 114). The stocking template is on page 125.

Heart decoration for the sausage dog draft excluder and the Christmas stocking

COWBOY HORSE

page 32

Horse's ear

STITCH KEY
You can follow this key or choose your own stitches.

■ French knot   ▦ Straight stitch   ▦ Seed stitch
▦ Backstitch   ▦ Chain and fly stitch ▦ Daisy stitch

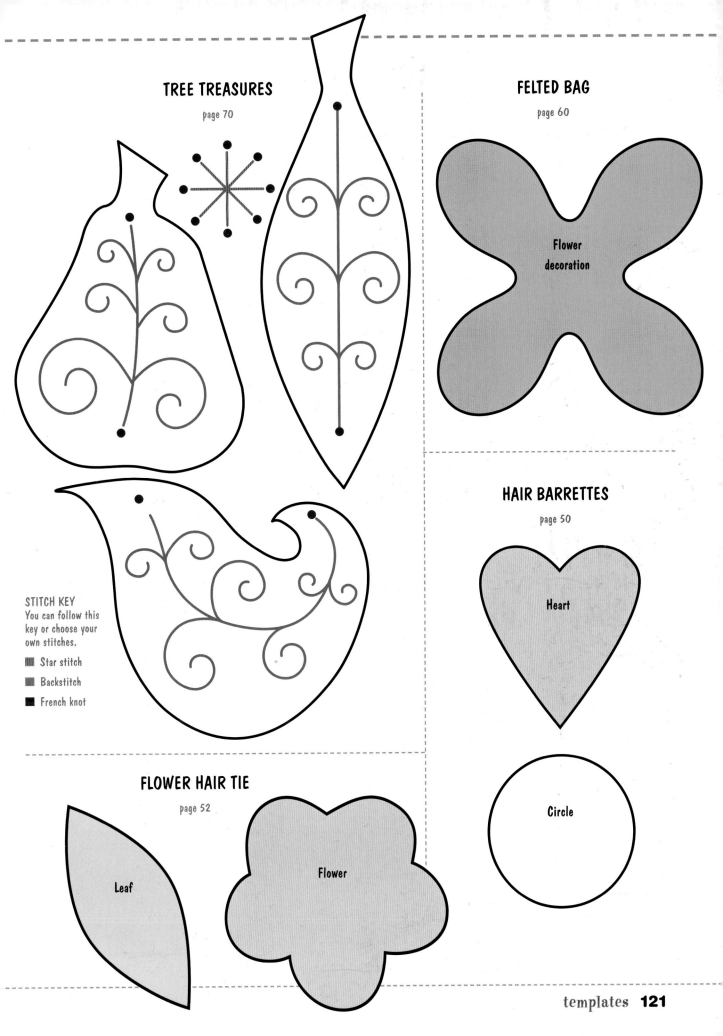

TREE TREASURES
page 70

FELTED BAG
page 60

Flower decoration

HAIR BARRETTES
page 50

Heart

Circle

STITCH KEY
You can follow this key or choose your own stitches.

▦ Star stitch
▨ Backstitch
● French knot

FLOWER HAIR TIE
page 52

Leaf

Flower

For instructions on how to use these templates, see page 114. All the templates on pages 122–123 are the correct size, so you can trace them.

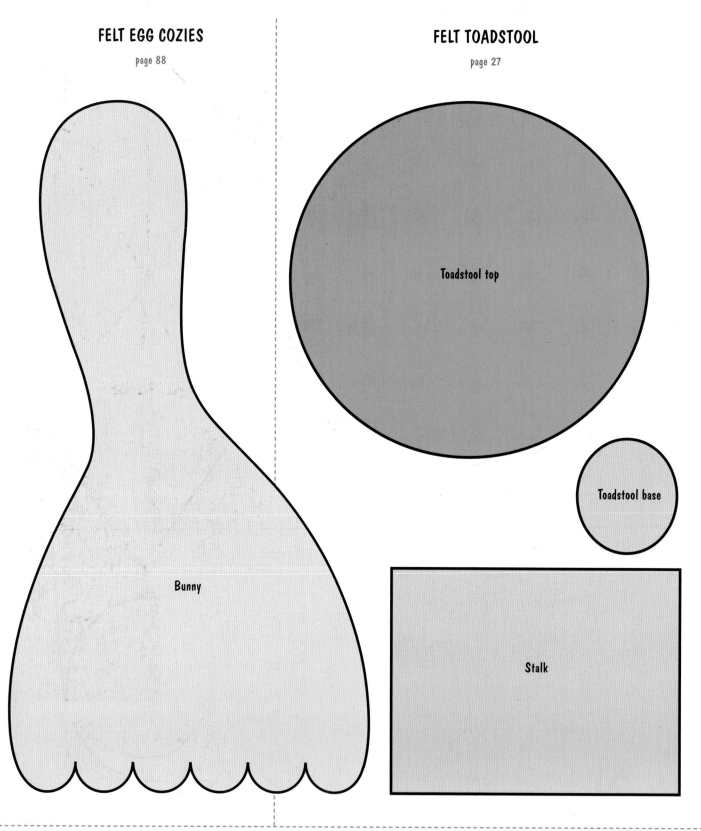

FELT EGG COZIES
page 88

Bunny

FELT TOADSTOOL
page 27

Toadstool top

Toadstool base

Stalk

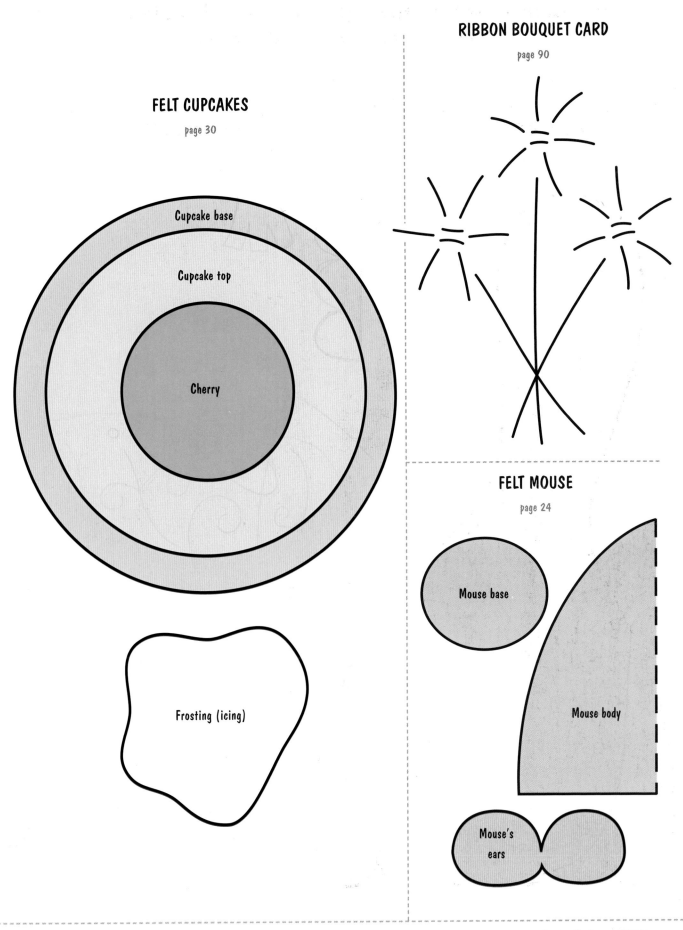

FELT CUPCAKES

page 30

Cupcake base

Cupcake top

Cherry

Frosting (icing)

RIBBON BOUQUET CARD

page 90

FELT MOUSE

page 24

Mouse base

Mouse body

Mouse's ears

For instructions on how to use these templates, see page 114. All the templates on pages 124–125 are half size and need to be doubled in size. Ask someone to help you photocopy them, using the 200% zoom button on the photocopier.

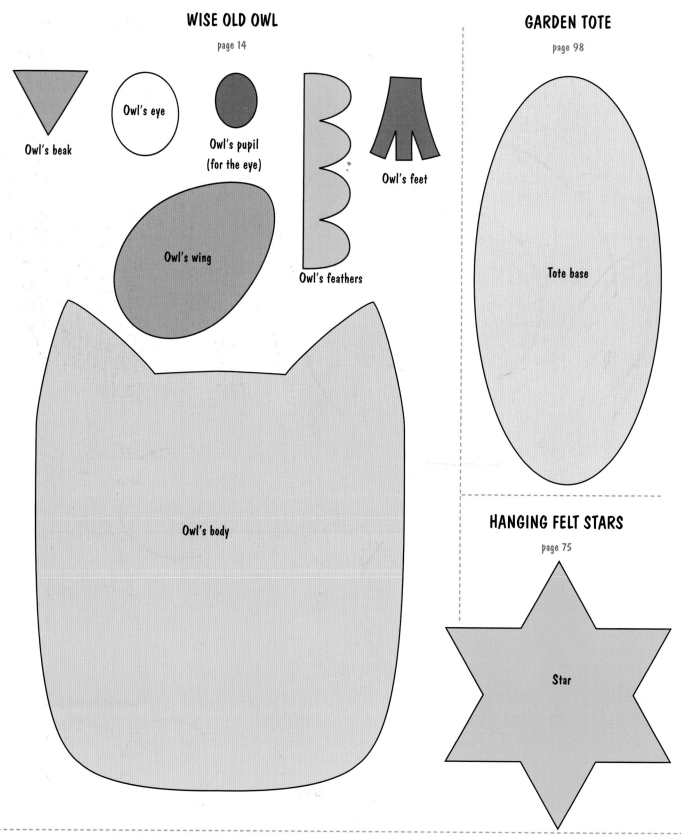

WISE OLD OWL

page 14

Owl's beak

Owl's eye

Owl's pupil
(for the eye)

Owl's feet

Owl's wing

Owl's feathers

Owl's body

GARDEN TOTE

page 98

Tote base

HANGING FELT STARS

page 75

Star

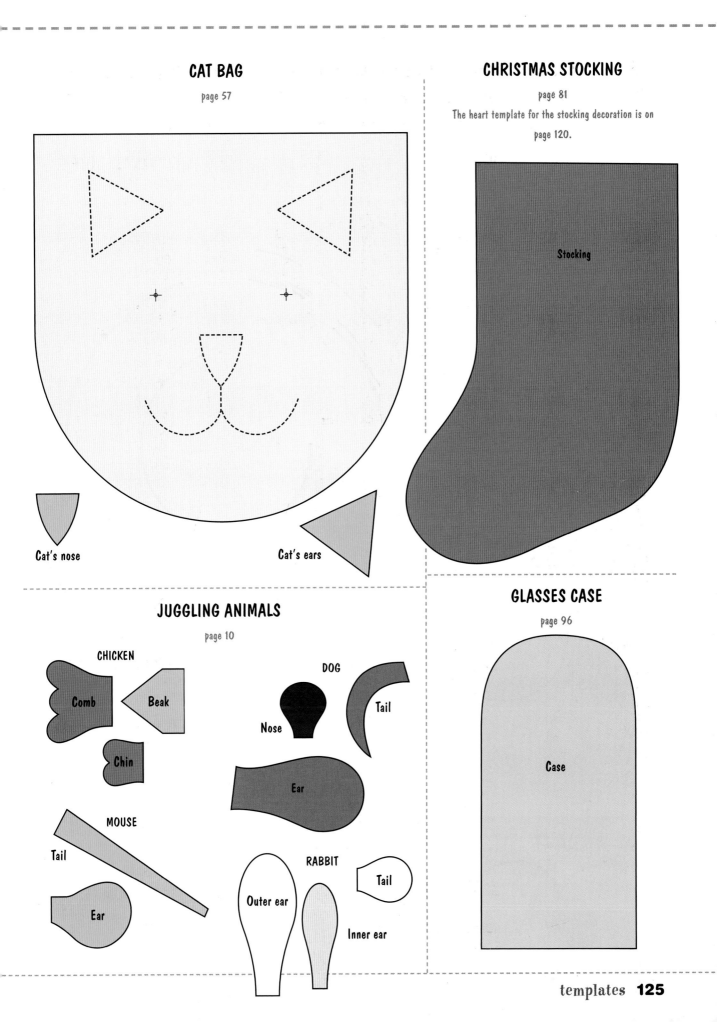

CAT BAG
page 57

Cat's nose

Cat's ears

CHRISTMAS STOCKING
page 81
The heart template for the stocking decoration is on page 120.

Stocking

JUGGLING ANIMALS
page 10

CHICKEN

Comb

Beak

Chin

DOG

Nose

Tail

Ear

MOUSE

Tail

Ear

RABBIT

Outer ear

Inner ear

Tail

GLASSES CASE
page 96

Case

For instructions on how to use these templates, see page 114. All the templates on pages 126—127 are half size and need to be doubled in size. Ask someone to help you photocopy them, using the 200% zoom button on the photocopier.

RAG DOLLS

page 34

DOLL'S CLOTHES

page 38

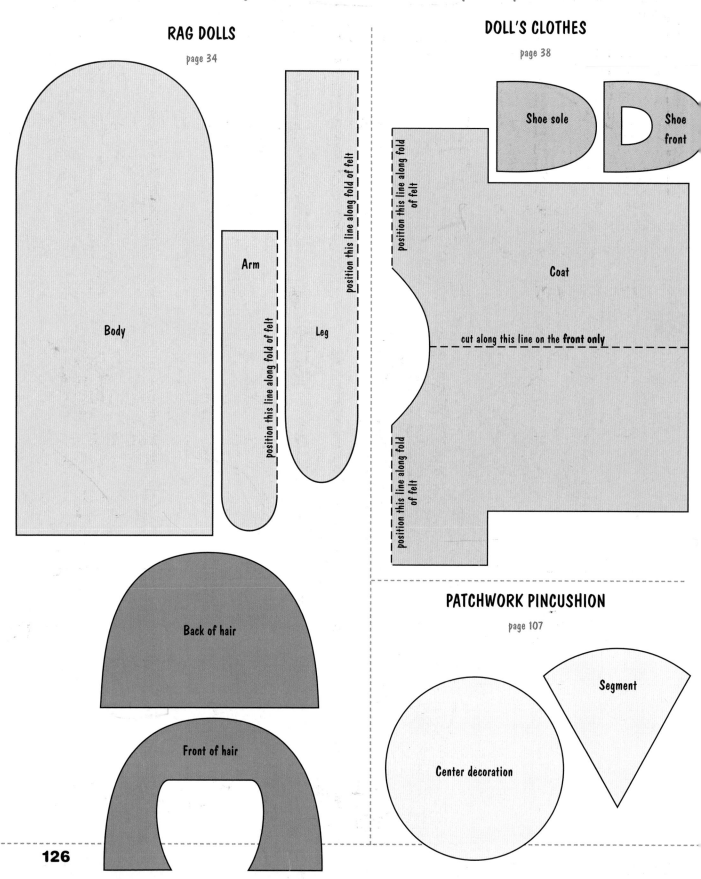

Body

Arm

position this line along fold of felt

Leg

position this line along fold of felt

Shoe sole

Shoe front

position this line along fold of felt

Coat

cut along this line on the **front only**

position this line along fold of felt

Back of hair

Front of hair

PATCHWORK PINCUSHION

page 107

Center decoration

Segment

FINGER PUPPET CARD

page 93

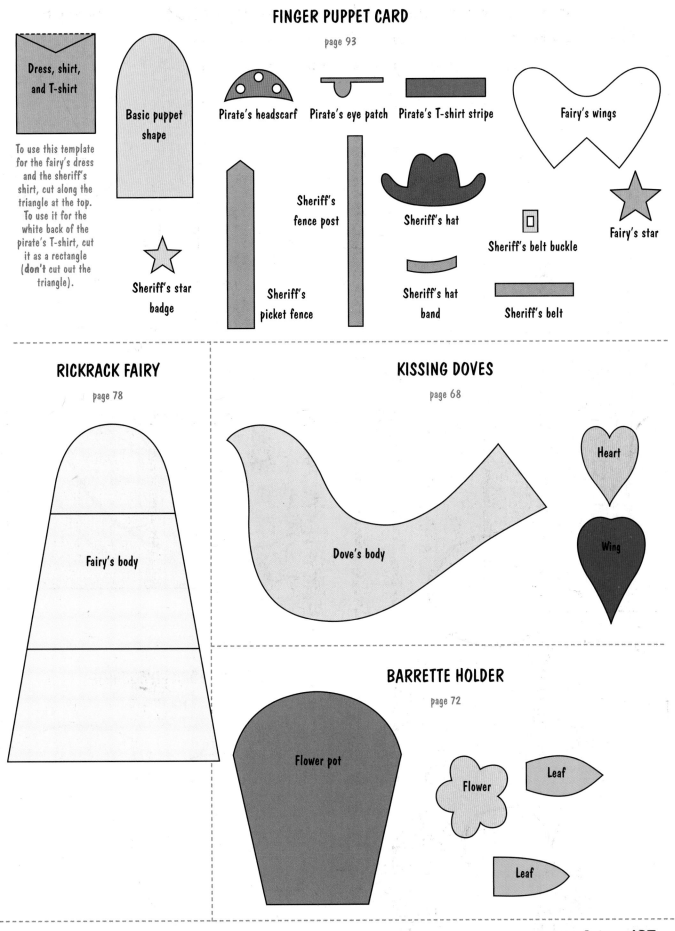

Dress, shirt, and T-shirt

To use this template for the fairy's dress and the sheriff's shirt, cut along the triangle at the top. To use it for the white back of the pirate's T-shirt, cut it as a rectangle (**don't** cut out the triangle).

Basic puppet shape

Sheriff's star badge

Pirate's headscarf

Pirate's eye patch

Pirate's T-shirt stripe

Fairy's wings

Sheriff's fence post

Sheriff's picket fence

Sheriff's hat

Sheriff's hat band

Sheriff's belt buckle

Sheriff's belt

Fairy's star

RICKRACK FAIRY

page 78

Fairy's body

KISSING DOVES

page 68

Dove's body

Heart

Wing

BARRETTE HOLDER

page 72

Flower pot

Flower

Leaf

Leaf

Index

Acknowledgments

Project makers
Tessa Evelegh: pages 68–69
Emma Hardy: pages 10–41, 50–65, 72–74, 78–80, 90–95, 101–113
Catherine Woram: pages 46–49, 75–77, 81–85, 88–89, 96–100
Clare Youngs: pages 44–45, 70–71

Photography
Caroline Arber: page 69
Emma Mitchell: pages 1, 89
Debbie Patterson: pages 2–4, 6–42, 51–66, 73, 79–80, 101–111
Claire Richardson: pages 43–45, 71
Tino Tedaldi: pages 86, 91–95,
Polly Wreford: pages 5, 47–49, 67, 77, 81–85, 97–99

Jacket photography: back cover and spine: Debbie Patterson; front cover: Debbie Patterson, Emma Mitchell (top far left), and Polly Wreford (bottom center)

Suppliers

US
A C Moore
www.acmoore.com

Create For Less
www.createforless.com

Hobby Lobby
www.hobbylobby.com

Jo-ann Fabric & Crafts
www.joann.com

Michaels
www.michaels.com

UK
Buttonbag
www.buttonbag.co.uk

Early Learning Centre
www.elc.co.uk

Homecrafts Direct
www.homecrafts.co.uk

Hobbycraft
www.hobbycraft.co.uk

John Lewis
www.johnlewis.co.uk